The Little Book
of Market Manipulation

An Essential Guide to the Law

Gregory J Durston and Ailsa McKeon

☆ WATERSIDE PRESS

The Little Book of Market Manipulation: An Essential Guide to the Law
Gregory J Durston and Alisa McKeon

ISBN 978-1-909976-73-3 (Paperback)
ISBN 978-1-910979-89-1 (Epub ebook)
ISBN 978-1-910979-90-7 (Adobe ebook)

Cover design © 2020 Waterside Press by www.gibgob.com

Printed by Severn, Gloucester, UK.

Main UK distributor Gardners Books, 1 Whittle Drive, Eastbourne, East Sussex, BN23 6QH. Tel: +44 (0)1323 521777; sales@gardners.com; www.gardners.com

North American distribution Ingram Book Company, One Ingram Blvd, La Vergne, TN 37086, USA. Tel: (+1) 615 793 5000; inquiry@ingramcontent.com

Cataloguing-In-Publication Data A catalogue record for this book can be obtained from the British Library.

Ebook *The Little Book of Market Manipulation* is available as an ebook and also to subscribers of Ebrary, Ebsco, Myilibrary and Dawsonera.

Published 2020 by
Waterside Press Ltd
Sherfield Gables
Sherfield on Loddon, Hook
Hampshire RG27 0JG.

Telephone +44(0)1256 882250
Online catalogue WatersidePress.co.uk
Email enquiries@watersidepress.co.uk

Contents

Publisher's note

The views and opinions expressed in this book are those of the authors entirely and not necessarily shared by the publisher. Readers should draw their own conclusions about any claims made or any facts or opinions stated concerning which the possibility of alternative interpretations, narratives, descriptions, subtleties of terminology or developments not sufficiently reported or in the public domain at the time of writing, or which may have occurred since that time should be borne in mind.

Acknowledgements

We would like to acknowledge the invaluable assistance provided by the staff at Kingston University Library, Southern Cross University Library, Lincoln's Inn Library, and the British Library. Additionally, we are extremely grateful for advice from Victor Temple QC and Judge Nicholas Philpot. Readers should note that abbreviated titles are sometimes used in footnotes; the full versions of these sources can be found in the *Select Bibliography*. Some newspaper citations refer to electronic editions.

Gregory Durston
Ailsa McKeon

London, January, 2020

About the authors

Gregory J Durston is a barrister who has taught law in England and Japan, having been Reader in Law at Kingston University, Surrey. The author of *Whores and Highwaymen: Crime and Justice in the Eighteenth-Century Metropolis* (hardback 2012; paperback 2016), *Fields, Fens and Felonies: Crime and Justice in Eighteenth-Century East Anglia* (2016) and *The Little Book of Insider Dealing* (2018) (with Mohsin Zaidi) (all Waterside Press), he is currently Adjunct Professor Southern Cross University School of Law and Justice, New South Wales, Australia.

Ailsa McKeon is a barrister at 6KBW College Hill. She holds a dual BA/LLB (Hons I) from the University of Queensland, Australia, where she initially qualified as a solicitor, going on to obtain a first in her LLM at Cambridge University. She has also worked in The Hague and the Turks and Caicos Islands.

CHAPTER 1

Introduction

Preliminary Matters

'Market abuse' is a generic term usually considered to entail two distinct forms of financial misconduct: insider dealing (including the unlawful disclosure of inside information) and market manipulation.[1] The former is dealt with in the companion volume to this work, *The Little Book of Insider Dealing*, to which reference will sometimes be made if only to avoid duplication. This concise guide considers market manipulation; that is, deliberate attempts to interfere with the proper operation of markets in financial instruments, securities, commodities and currencies, by artificially inflating or deflating their price, usually in order to benefit from such effects.[2]

As with the previous volume, this book focuses on the more significant and commonly encountered aspects of market manipulation, rather than its more recondite areas. As a result, rarely seen forms of manipulation, such as 'cornering' the market[3] or its less drastic cousin 'the squeeze'[4] are not examined. It is hoped that this brief work will provide a succinct but accurate introduction to the field that also facilitates comprehension of the major

---

1   Market Abuse Regulation (EU) No. 596/2014, as amended at recital (7).

2   Shaun D Ledgerwood and Jeremy A Verlinda, 'Derivatives' Roles in Manipulation' (2017) 27(9) *Futures and Derivatives Law Report* 1.

3   That is, obtaining sufficient dominance over supply in a particular security to allow its price to be artificially set.

4   This refers to obtaining enough control over the supply of a financial instrument to have some impact on its price, albeit not to the same extent as occurs with 'cornering the market'.

practitioner texts in this complicated but highly topical area of the law.[5]

Regulatory Frameworks for Market Manipulation

There are several frameworks within which market manipulation constitutes wrongful conduct. This work is primarily concerned with the criminal and regulatory offences currently in force. An overview of these is the focus of much of this chapter. However, civil actions and the impact of various principles laid out by the Financial Conduct Authority (FCA) in its *Handbook* also bear brief mention.

Criminal and Regulatory Offences

The current regime of criminal offences dealing with market manipulation is set out in sections 89 to 91 of the Financial Services Act 2012 (FSA 2012), which is explained in detail in the chapters that follow. This is supplemented, albeit rarely in practice, by the common law and potentially also the Fraud Act 2006.

The regulatory offence is set out in article 15 of the Market Abuse Regulation (MAR)[6] which, under the heading 'Prohibition of market manipulation', simply states: '*A person shall not engage in or attempt to engage in market manipulation*'. Further elaboration is given by the lengthy article 12.

Each of the key provisions referred to here is set out in full in the *Appendix* to this work.

Breadth of Coverage

As will be seen, the criminal and regulatory market manipulation regimes in the UK govern a large (and growing) list of financial instruments. These include commodity futures, emissions allowances, gilts and equities, among many others. In the modern era, much market manipulation also involves

---

5   These include Karen Anderson et al's authoritative text, *A Practitioner's Guide to the Law and Regulation of Market Abuse* (2017, Sweet & Maxwell, 2nd edn.). Barry Rider et al's *Market Abuse and Insider Dealing* (2016, Bloomsbury Professional, 3rd edn.) is well worth reading. The most recent major work in the field is Edward Swan and John Virgo's *Market Abuse Regulation* (2019, Oxford University Press). Janet Austin's *Insider Trading and Market Manipulation: Investigating and Prosecuting Across Borders* (2017, Edward Elgar) provides a valuable international perspective.

6   (EU) No. 596/2014, as amended.

the use of 'derivatives', which also fall within the remit of the regulatory and criminal regimes.

Derivatives are financial instruments that derive their value from that of an underlying asset. Some such assets are tangible, like agricultural commodities, while others are intangible, such as shares and currencies. Derivatives allow contracting parties to assume a trading position on the future movements of the underlying asset. Those who hold them will be afforded a particular set of rights and obligations, depending on the nature of the derivative. Parties investing in derivatives often hope to profit from price changes in the underlying asset, whether as speculation or as a hedge against an unfavourable change in the market.[7]

Manipulation is not proscribed at large, but is prohibited on a diverse list of markets and exchanges such as the London International Financial Futures and Options Exchange (LIFFE), the London Metal Exchange (LME), and the London Stock Exchange (LSE). The LSE is one of the most common forums for such misbehaviour, whether on its Main Market (MM) or, even more frequently, its Alternative Investment Market (AIM). As a result, shares traded on the LSE will often be treated as the exemplar in this book.

Although the majority of share trading in companies listed in the UK still takes place on the LSE, the Markets in Financial Instruments Directive (MiFID) of November 2007 (revised by MiFID II in January 2018) allowed other bodies to set up their own electronic trading platforms. These are usually known as Multilateral Trading Facilities (MTFs). Market manipulation can occur on these platforms, just as it can on the LSE's markets. More generally, and as FCA officials have stressed, any assumption that market abuse (including manipulation) only happens with regard to equities is seriously mistaken.[8]

Although this work considers the situation in the UK (both criminal and

---

7   Anna Chadwick, 'Gambling on Hunger? The Right to Adequate Food and Commodity Derivatives Trading' (2018) 18(2) *Human Rights Law Review* 233–265 at 240.

8   Julia Hoggett, 'Market Abuse Requires a Dynamic Response to a Changing Risk Profile' (speech delivered at Association for Financial Markets in Europe (AFME) Implementation of the Market Abuse Regulation in the UK Event, London, 13 February 2019); https://www.fca.org.uk/news/speeches/market-abuse-requires-dynamic-response-changing-risk-profile (Hoggett, 'Dynamic Response').

regulatory regimes operate nationwide), with particular reference to England and Wales, some comparison and reference will necessarily be made with other jurisdictions. This is not least because the rapid globalisation of securities markets has made manipulation an international problem which increasingly crosses national borders and so occasions difficulties for those tasked with investigating and punishing such behaviour.[9]

It has been suggested that the International Organization of Securities Commissions (IOSCO), the Madrid-based body on which most of the world's securities regulators are represented, should be more powerful and proactive in liaising with, and coordinating the activities of, national securities' regulators, to deal with this expanding problem.[10] To that end, IOSCO established a Multilateral Memorandum of Understanding Concerning Consultation and Cooperation and the Exchange of Information in May 2002. This was revised in May 2012 and is still the primary instrument employed by regulators around the world when seeking international assistance in enforcing securities laws and regulations. Furthermore, in June 2013, IOSCO established a Task Force on Cross-Border Regulation, which reported in September 2015.[11] That report included the development of a Cross-Border Regulatory Toolkit, of which there has been a significant and successful uptake. IOSCO nonetheless remains seized of cross-border cooperation issues in light of continuous market evolution.[12]

Closer to home, however, the MAR has 'direct effect' in the UK as a European Union regulation. It will also continue in effect after the UK's departure from the EU by virtue of the European Union (Withdrawal) Act 2018 (Withdrawal Act) and the Market Abuse (Amendment) (EU Exit) Regulations 2019, SI No. 310 (Exit Regulations), if and when brought into

---

9   Janet Austin, *Insider Trading and Market Manipulation: Investigating and Prosecuting Across Borders* (2017, Edward Elgar) at 1–2.

10 See generally, Janet Austin, *When Insider Trading and Market Manipulation Cross Jurisdictions. What Are the Challenges for Securities Regulators and How Can They Best Preserve the Integrity of Markets?* (2016, PhD Thesis — University of York (Toronto)); https://digitalcommons.osgoode. yorku.ca/cgi/viewcontent.cgi?referer=&httpsredir=1&article=1021&context=phd

11 See IOSCO Task Force on Cross-Border Regulation, *Final Report* (2015); https://www.iosco. org/library/pubdocs/pdf/IOSCOPD507.pdf

12 See IOSCO, *Market Fragmentation & Cross-border Regulation* (2019); https://www.iosco.org/ library/pubdocs/pdf/IOSCOPD629.pdf

force—many provisions come into effect on 'exit day'.[13] Section 1 of the Withdrawal Act repeals the European Communities Act 1972 and converts the existing body of directly applicable EU law into UK domestic law. The Financial Services and Markets Act 2000 (Amendment) (EU Exit) Regulations 2019 grant the current regulator, the FCA, the power to make transitional directions to mitigate disruption caused by exit-related changes to regulated firms' obligations.

All this aside, it is highly unlikely that the UK will in future maintain a market abuse regime that is not at least as strict as that formulated by the EU. The UK's current criminal regime is more robust than that found in most other European countries or required by the EU, hence the decision not to adopt the EU criminal sanctions regime.[14] In this regard, at least, the UK's departure from the EU ought not to cause too much disruption.

Civil Actions

Market manipulation involving misleading representations may also be the basis for civil actions brought to recoup victims' losses. There are three obvious bases on which such a claim could be framed by an investor at large: first, for negligent misstatement under the restrictive principles set out by the House of Lords in *Hedley Byrne & Co Ltd v Heller & Partners Ltd* (1964) AC 465; secondly, for the tort of deceit, as defined in *Derry v Peek* (1889) 14 App Cas 337; and thirdly, where the conduct occurs against the backdrop of a contractual agreement, for negligent misstatement under section 2(1) of the Misrepresentation Act 1967.[15]

Civil liability is also created or reinforced by certain provisions of the Financial Services and Markets Act 2000 (FSMA), which governs many aspects of financial services in the UK, alongside FSA 2012. Section 90 FSMA creates liability to compensate individuals who have acquired securities and suffered loss on the basis that the securities' listing particulars contained

---

13   See Exit Regulations, regulation 1(3).

14   See Mark Hoban (Financial Secretary to the Treasury), Ministerial Statement to the House of Commons: 'Criminal Sanctions Directive on Market Abuse', 20 February 2012; https://publications.parliament.uk/pa/cm201212/cmhansrd/cm120220/wmstext/120220m0001.htm

15   Anderson et al, *A Practitioner's Guide*, at 171–75.

untrue or misleading statements, omitted matters required by legislation, or were not amended where legislation so required. Section 90A has the same effect in connection with information published on a recognised information service, such as the LSE's Regulatory News Service (RNS).[16] As such, it is not only the response of official regulators of which intending market manipulators need to be aware.

FCA Handbook

Last in the hierarchy of market manipulation regulations are the targeted principles set out in the FCA's *Handbook*. The *Handbook* contains all legal instruments created by the FCA pursuant to its rule-making powers in FSMA and regulations thereunder.

The *Handbook* addresses various different topics. Of most relevance to market manipulation are three of its High Level Standards, namely the Principles for Business (PRIN), the Code of Conduct (COCON), and the Statements of Principle and Code of Practice for Approved Persons (APER). In the present context, the Business Standards on Market Conduct (MARC) are also important to note.[17]

The Principles for Business set out the fundamental obligations of regulated persons and are linked to the concept of being a 'fit and proper person' for the purposes of FSMA.[18] Of the ten principles, market manipulation is likely to engage principles 1 and 5, which respectively require that a firm 'must conduct its business with integrity' and 'observe proper standards of market conduct'.[19] Rules 1 and 5 of the Code of Conduct, and Statements of Principle 1 and 3, mirror these principles but respectively apply to individuals and 'approved persons'.[20]

Each set of obligations applies to specific types of person regulated by the FCA, rather than at large. Such persons may face disciplinary sanctions, including financial penalties, public censure, or withdrawal of authorisation

---

16 Ibid.
17 See PRIN 1.1.7 and SUP 15.11.
18 See PRIN 1.1.4.
19 See PRIN 2.1.
20 See COCON 2.1 and APER 2.1A.3. Detail as to the substance of the Statements of Principle is contained in APER 4.1 and 4.3.

or approval, for breach of the applicable standards—an individualised disincentive from engaging in market manipulation.

History and Rationale for Proscription of Market Manipulation

Having set out in broad brush what market manipulation means today, it is worthwhile examining how this point has been reached. It is also particularly important to understand the rationale for proscribing market manipulation. The purpose behind a transaction is often the deciding factor between whether it was manipulative or not—without proper context, a seemingly fickle distinction.

A Neglected Phenomenon

To a degree, scrutiny of market manipulation has been neglected in favour of its better-known cousin, insider dealing. As Julia Hoggett, the FCA's Director of Market Oversight, noted in November 2017, insider dealing is the 'poster-child of market abuse', while market manipulation remains in the background.[21]

In part, this may be because insider dealing appears to be much more common. For example, since 2016 the MAR has mandated the making of suspicious transaction and order reports (STORs; discussed further below) where questionable activities come to the attention of certain market operators. In recent years, over 80% of STORs submitted to the FCA have concerned insider dealing, while fewer than 20% have addressed market manipulation. In 2018, the number was just 812, as compared with 5,107 for insider dealing.[22]

In addition, empirical research on market manipulation is still quite

---

21 Julia Hoggett, 'Effective Compliance with the Market Abuse Regulation—A State of Mind' (speech delivered at Recent Developments in the Market Abuse Regime Conference, London, 14 November 2017); https://www.fca.org.uk/news/speeches/effective-compliance-market-abuse-regulation-a-state-of-mind (Hoggett, 'Effective Compliance').

22 See FCA, 'Number of STORs Received: 2018', 13 February 2019; https://www.fca.org.uk/markets/suspicious-transaction-and-order-reports/number-stors-received-2018

limited everywhere in the world.[23] Although the academic literature shows that it occurs on a wide variety of markets, how frequently market manipulation takes place remains highly uncertain. Some observers suspect that it is very much more common and widespread than is appreciated. It appears that only a small fraction of market manipulation is detected, let alone prosecuted.[24] Whatever its incidence, it is a matter of considerable importance for all investors.

The Rationale for Proscription

Market manipulation results in market participants either buying or selling at worse prices than they could otherwise have achieved. Such participants include those who deal on behalf of pension funds, for example: it is not merely professional investors who may lose out. And such losses are not only costly for individuals whose money is invested. Markets rely on those who trade on them having faith in appropriate price formation taking place, just as they do in investors believing that price sensitive information will not be abused by insider dealing. Such confidence encourages liquidity and so investment. Combatting market manipulation is vital to ensuring that such confidence is preserved.[25]

That was precisely the sentiment expressed by His Honour Judge Elwen when sentencing former AIT directors Carl Rigby and Gareth Bailey for market manipulation in 2005: 'Every member of the public, having savings by direct investment on the stock market or by and through products themselves tied to stock markets, is injured if the integrity of the market is damaged by misleading information of this kind being announced to the market'. He also noted that the health of the financial services industry, a major contributor to the UK's economy, suffered by such conduct.[26] More

---

23 Nonetheless, for an analysis outside the UK or US, see Dewa Gede Wirama et al, 'Price Manipulation by Dissemination of Rumours: Evidence from the Indonesian Stock Market' (2017) 7(1) *International Journal of Economics and Financial Issues* 429–434.

24 Talis J Putnin, 'Market Manipulation: A Survey' (2012) 26(5) *Journal of Economic Surveys* 952–967 at 953.

25 Hoggett, 'Effective Compliance'.

26 As reported in, e.g. *Citywire*, 7 October 2005; https://citywire.co.uk/wealth-manager/news/city-taught-a-tough-lesson-as-former-ait-directors-go-to-prison/a269197?ref=author/jwallen

recently, scrutiny of the causes of the global financial crisis of 2007 to 2009 has identified white-collar crime, including market manipulation, as a key contributory factor.

History of Market Manipulation

One could be forgiven for thinking market manipulation is a modern phenomenon, but in fact it is as old as trading on organized exchanges itself. The Amsterdam Stock Exchange—the world's first—was opened in 1602. Just seven years later, in 1609, Isaac le Maire (1558–1624), a major entrepreneur and investor in The Netherlands, conducted what is recognised as the first bear raid.[27] He suddenly sold all of his Dutch East India Company stock, forcing its price sharply down, and then repurchased it at an advantageous rate.

Similarly, Joseph de la Vega's descriptions of the Amsterdam Stock Exchange in the late seventeenth century in his *Confusion de Confusiones* lists a variety of strategies used by the speculators of his day, many of which would now be considered market manipulation. Amongst them were early examples of 'painting the tape': conducting false trades to convey the illusion of activity in an investment.[28]

Numerous cases of manipulation occurred in ensuing centuries, including, very famously, the Rothschilds' supposed sale of large amounts of stock in London to create the false impression that Napoleon had defeated Wellington. This caused prices to crash and allegedly allowed the banking family to repurchase the stock at depressed prices.[29] A little further on again, Daniel Drew (1797–1879), an American financier, became notorious for manipulation during the nineteenth century, deliberately spreading unfounded rumours to affect stock prices. In the 1920s, what were then termed 'stock pools' were widespread in the USA, attracting prominent men such as Joseph Kennedy to their ranks and engaging in quite overt manipulation. A group of investors who owned large amounts of stock in a particular company,

---

27 Murray Sayle, 'Japan Goes Dutch', (2001) 23(7) *London Review of Books* 3–7.

28 David Leinweber and Ananth Madhavan, 'Three Hundred Years of Stock Market Manipulation' (2001) 10(2) *Journal of Investing* 7–16 at 3.

29 Putnin, 'Market Manipulation', at 956.

acting in concert, might sell a small number of shares back and forth to each other at successively higher prices, so 'walking the stock up' before disposing of a large tranche at favourable rates. For example, in 1929, the so-called 'Radio Pool' coordinated share purchases to send the phonograph manufacturer RCA's shares to an absurd $549 each. That price would not be genuinely matched by the company until the 1960s. Ironically, after making a small fortune in this manner, Joseph Kennedy was in 1934 made the first chairman of the Securities and Exchange Commission (SEC), which sought to crack down on such previously-legal practices.[30]

The SEC was created by Congress after the stock market crash of 1929, which precipitated the Great Depression in the USA and revealed the weakness of its existing regulatory framework. This was comprised both of self-regulation within the securities industries and a patchwork of state laws, which varied among jurisdictions. Neither offered more than minimal protection for investors. In tandem with his New Deal, addressing this situation was a key priority of President F D Roosevelt when he came into office in 1933.[31] Although the original Securities Exchange Act 1934 (also known as the Glass-Steagall Act) was repealed in 1999,[32] in the interim it paved the way for the development of market regulation in the US and beyond.

Attractions of Market Manipulation

The essential attraction of market manipulation is that, even in its simplest forms, it can lead to swift and substantial profits. For example, in 2000, two young graduates of the University of California, Los Angeles, pleaded guilty to securities fraud for having earlier run a crude 'pump and dump' scheme.[33] They had bought thousands of shares in a small and struggling commercial printing company, NEI Webworld Inc, then inflated its share price by making postings to the OTC Bulletin Board. Those postings suggested that the company would be the subject of an imminent takeover bid,

30 John H Davis, *The Kennedys: Dynasty and Disaster, 1848–1983* (1984) at 56.
31 See generally Anne M Khademian, *The SEC and Capital Market Regulation: The Politics of Expertise* (1992, University of Pittsburgh Press) at 23–45.
32 Barry Eichengreen, *House of Mirrors: The Great Depression, the Great Recession, and the Uses and Misuses of History* (2016, Oxford University Press) at 11.
33 See *Chapter 2*.

which was entirely false. Influenced by these messages, at a time when this form of communication was still fairly novel, the price of the stock went from well under $1 up to $15.50 a share. This allowed the graduates to sell their holdings at a profit of nearly $350,000 before the share value again fell to just a few cents.[34]

The Influence of Technology

The above example is illustrative of the vast impact that technological developments have had, and continue to have, on stock markets worldwide. In Joseph De La Vega's time, an intending manipulator often had to go from coffee shop to coffee shop, regularly repeating unfounded rumours for them to have any effect on the market. Later, however, the emergence of newspapers and, more particularly, telephones allowed potentially gullible investors to be reached more easily and in greater numbers.[35] Sometimes cold calls were made from so-called 'boiler rooms', often to potential customers selected from telephone directories, lists of shareholders and the like, using high-pressure sales techniques designed to force victims into making decisions without due consideration. These calls might promote certain shares without disclosing the promoters' motives in doing so.[36] At other times, a single trader might make calls from his or her personal telephone to influential industry contacts, permitting misinformation to be spread via their onward communications.

More recently, the emergence of (spam) email, texting, social media, online investment chatrooms and noticeboards have given many manipulative stratagems a new impetus. Nowadays, spreading false information can be done much more easily and inexpensively, to a far wider audience, and

---

34 Indraneel Sur, '2 Plead Guilty in Internet Stock Fraud', *Los Angeles Times*, 7 July 2000; https://www.latimes.com/archives/la-xpm-2000-jul-07-fi-48902-story.html; US SEC, 'SEC Files New and Expanded Charges Against Two Defendants in NEI Webworld Internet Stock Manipulation Case; Both Plead Guilty to Criminal Charges', Litigation Release No. 16620, 6 July 2000 https://www.sec.gov/litigation/litreleases/lr16620.htm

35 David Leinweber and Ananth Madhavan, 'Three Hundred Years of Stock Market Manipulation' (2001) 10(2) *Journal of Investing* 7–16 at 13.

36 Paul Barnes, 'Stock Market Scams, Shell Companies, Penny Shares, Boiler Rooms and Cold Calling: The UK Experience' (2017) 48 *International Journal of Law, Crime and Justice* 50–64 at 51.

with much more anonymity for the fraudster than was previously the case. Unsurprisingly, the SEC has urged that '… investors who learn of investing opportunities from social media should always be on the lookout for fraud'.[37]

Similarly, forms of manipulation that rely on giving a misleading impression to other traders via transactions (apparent or real) have been greatly facilitated by technological developments over recent decades. These include the establishment of complex electronic exchanges and markets since the 1980s, and, even more significantly, the emergence of high-frequency trading (HFT) after the millennium. HFT essentially comprises the use of powerful semi-autonomous supercomputers to transact large numbers of orders at very fast speeds, often using sophisticated algorithms with automated, pre-programmed trading instructions. These can analyse multiple markets before buying and selling, without traders having to make orders manually. Tiny periods of time — literally milliseconds — can therefore be vital to placing and withdrawing orders, and significant movements in market prices can be correspondingly fast.[38]

To exploit this, some high-frequency traders install ultra-fast fibre-optic data connections between their systems and modern stock exchanges, giving them a minuscule speed advantage over rivals. For example, in 2010, millions of dollars were spent laying the most direct fibre-optic cable between a data centre in Chicago and the New York Stock Exchange, a distance of some 827 miles, reducing the journey-time of data from 17 to 13 milliseconds.[39] Although just thousandths of a second, this added speed allows the traders to see and react to other buyers' orders before execution.

HFT now accounts for a large amount of trading on stock exchanges. By 2015 it made up 60% of deals in the USA and about 30% in the UK. It is also found on most other exchanges.[40] It is not only used for trading equities, but also foreign exchange and commodities, albeit to a more modest

---

37   See e.g. 'Updated Investor Alert: Social Media and Investing-Stock Rumors', 5 November 2015; https://www.sec.gov/oiea/investor-alerts-bulletins/ia_rumors.html

38   See generally, Scott Patterson, *Dark Pools: The Rise of Artificially Intelligent Trading Machines and the Looming Threat to Wall Street* (2012, Random House).

39   Michael Lewis, *Flash Boys* (2014, WW Norton & Co) at 10–22.

40   Jonathan Fisher et al, 'Criminal Forms of High Frequency Trading on the Financial Markets' (2015) 9(2) *Law and Financial Markets Review* 113–119 at 113.

degree. Although HFT is not, of course, manipulative *per se*, the speed at which transactions occur can facilitate manipulative conduct, as well as making it more difficult to detect.

As a result of such developments, the popular image of the New York Stock Exchange, with its real-time tickers and bankers, is something of an illusion. In reality, much dealing takes place far away from Wall Street, via supercomputers connected by fibre optic cables, through which billions of dollars can move in seconds. Today it seems that relatively small numbers of actors can manipulate huge financial markets with the simple click of a button. The City of London is probably little different. However, as the FCA's director of enforcement noted in 2019, although the regulator cannot prosecute a computer, it can take action against those who provided its governance.[41]

Vulnerability to Market Manipulation

Not all shares, securities, and financial instruments are equally at risk of manipulation. Few, however, are immune to it. For example, the electronic Forex (FX) market had a turnover of $5.3 trillion daily in April 2013.[42] This massive size makes it a difficult forum to manipulate, especially where major currencies are involved. For a long time, regulators thought it was simply too large for manipulation to occur.

Nonetheless, in 2014, six major banks were fined a total of £2.6bn by UK and US regulators over their traders' manipulation of foreign exchange rates.[43] It was said that the traders had manipulated foreign exchange benchmarks by making trades just before and during the 60-second windows when the benchmarks were set (a manipulative trading practice known as 'banging the close'). They reportedly liaised with each other using online messaging services, and chat names such as 'The Cartel' and 'The Bandits' Club'. The FCA proceeded down the regulatory route, so there were no

---

41 Hoggett, 'Dynamic Response'.

42 See Bank for International Settlements, *Triennial Central Bank Survey—Foreign Exchange Turnover in April 2013: Preliminary Global Results;* https://www.bis.org/publ/rpfxi3fx.pdf at 3.

43 Jill Treanor, 'Foreign Exchange Fines: Banks Handed £2.6bn in Penalties for Market Rigging', *The Guardian*, 12 November 2014; https://www.theguardian.com/business/2014/nov/12/foreign-exchange-fines-ubs-hsbc-citibank-jp-morgan-rbs-penalties-market-rigging

criminal prosecutions in the UK and only one arrest following a Serious Fraud Office (SFO) investigation (no charges were brought). A number of finance professionals were dismissed from their employment in the aftermath.[44] Nonetheless, fresh fines were imposed on five institutions by the EU's competition watchdog for similar activities in 2019.[45]

On the other hand, cheaply-priced and thinly-traded equities, such as so called 'penny shares',[46] are particularly vulnerable to manipulative schemes. This is due to their low values, the lack of easily accessible information about their issuers, their general lack of liquidity, and their wide 'spread' (that is, the difference between the amount it costs to buy and to sell these securities). This means that, for example, if a share is trading at 1p and a promoter can move its price to 2p, they will, theoretically, have doubled the value of the holding.

Stocks that trade on smaller indexes, such as the LSE's AIM, also tend to be more thinly traded than those larger markets, so that they are often more vulnerable to manipulation as well. A relatively small number of buys or sells in one direction can sometimes produce a significant movement in price. Of course, trading in penny shares and on the AIM can be (and frequently is) combined, as the former are disproportionately found on the latter.

It has been claimed that a handful of the thousand or so companies on the AIM are being 'pumped and dumped' at any one time. This is less than is sometimes suggested — unsuccessful investors frequently blame manipulation for their losses — but it occurs more commonly than on the MM. These stocks often share two features. They normally have a market capitalisation of less than £30m, and so limited numbers of shares, which means that their price will move swiftly with any liquidity. Furthermore, they are often found in a sector that naturally attracts speculation, such as 'blue-sky' technology stocks, with the attendant allure of potentially dramatic gains

---

44 Lamiat Sabin, 'Banker Arrested in Foreign Exchange Rigging Scandal after Banks Fined £2.6bn', *The Independent*, 20 December 2014; https://www.independent.co.uk/news/uk/crime/banker-arrested-in-foreign-exchange-rigging-scandal-after-banks-fined-26bn-9937469.html

45 Rochelle Toplensky, 'EU Fines Five Banks €1bn over Foreign Exchange Cartel', *The Financial Times*, 16 May 2019; < https://www.ft.com/content/73163fa0-77c5-11e9-bbad-7c18c0ea0201

46 In the US, this definition extends to those priced at up to $5 per share.

in value, making them attractive to gullible investors.[47]

For the same reason, and as the FCA has expressly noted, the relatively small size, and the limited number of specialist participants in niche markets such as, for example, the Robusta coffee futures and options market on LIFFE, means that they are particularly vulnerable to price manipulation.[48] The vast market for wheat would, by contrast, be much harder to manipulate.

Proving Manipulative Behaviour

Distinguishing manipulative behaviour from legitimate trading can be quite difficult, and proving it in a forensic environment, especially a criminal forum, even harder. More specifically, it can be particularly challenging to establish that the price of a security has been deliberately and artificially moved in a certain direction, in the absence of direct evidence of the defendant's state of mind, such as a recorded phone call, a preserved email, or a confession in interview. There might be entirely legitimate reasons for a trader's willingness to incur losses, or explanations for making bad bargains on specific transactions that also have a wider effect on the market. These might range from personal foolishness to a need for immediate liquidation or procurement of the asset being traded.[49]

For example, some observers, both traders and academics, have suggested that a significant part of the huge increase in value of the crypto-currency Bitcoin in 2017, from a low of under $780 to a high of over $19,700, was due to coordinated price manipulation. It has been said that Tether (USDT), another crypto-currency asset the value of which is supposed to be tethered to the US dollar, was used to make purchases of Bitcoin following market downturns in its value, preventing these turning into major falls. However, others have argued that such purchases are not necessarily proof of market

---

47   Gavin Rooke, 'A Dummies' Guide to Spotting a Pump and Dump on AIM', 24 April 2017;
     https://shareinvestors.co.uk/2017/04/24/a-dummies-guide-to-spotting-a-pump-and-dump-on-aim/

48   FSA, *Final Notice*, 1 June 2010.

49   Shaun D Ledgerwood and Paul R Carpenter, 'A Framework for the Analysis of Market Manipulation' (2012) *Review of Law and Economics* 253–295 at 255.

manipulation.[50] They could be explained by, *inter alia*, ordinary demand from traders 'buying the dip' and using lower prices to purchase a target security in the expectation that the fall will be followed by an upturn. (In any event, Bitcoin and other forms of cryptocurrency are not normally regulated by the FCA at present.)

Furthermore, today's market manipulators are often very good at concealing their schemes. For example, dishonest traders sometimes work together on a deal-by-deal basis, one helping the other in a scheme to manipulate the market in order to obtain the latter's co-operation in a separate future operation. Establishing a link between the two can be hard, as money never changes hands. When it comes to manipulation effected by misleading statements, it can be difficult to establish where the information originated once the manipulative enterprise is underway.

Additionally, and more generally, criminal trials for market manipulation are often long, while the evidence may not be 'jury-friendly': frequently, the prosecution will adduce the electronic fruits of market surveillance. Southwark Crown Court, the main forum for the trial of high-level white-collar crime in England and Wales, has been equipped for just this purpose, with jury computers and tablets. Nevertheless, it can still be difficult to put such evidence before juries in an effective manner, and by no means straightforward even with a regulatory action heard in the Upper Tribunal (Tax and Chancery Chamber) (UT(TCC)).

Despite these difficulties, the remainder of this book examines the basics of how a market manipulation case may progress in the regulatory and criminal arenas, starting with the many forms that this behaviour may take.

---

50   Matt Robinson and Tom Schoenberg, 'Bitcoin-Rigging Criminal Probe Focused on Tie to Tether' *Bloomberg*, 20 November 2018; https://www.bloomberg.com/news/articles/2018-11-20/bitcoin-rigging-criminal-probe-is-said-to-focus-on-tie-to-tether

CHAPTER 2

Forms of Market Manipulation

Setting the Scene

All financial markets, and the individual securities traded on them, are in a state of constant flux. Prices go up and down, sometimes dramatically, due to a huge range of entirely legitimate factors. For example, bad news, such as a company making a major loss, will see its share price fall on the LSE. Conversely, good news, such as the company securing a major contract, will drive it up. Bad weather at a sensitive time of year for growing coffee, in places where such production is concentrated, might lead to futures for certain types of regionally sourced coffee going up on LIFFE, while bountiful harvests can result in a fall.

However, the subject matter of this book is the artificial engineering of moves in security prices. Such artifice will usually make it appear as though the market is simply responding to the natural laws of supply and demand, when in fact the shifts are unrelated to the impact of extrinsic events on the collective judgement of buyers and sellers. There are a variety of motivations for this kind of conduct. Most obvious is the individual's immediate financial gain. Other reasons may include, for example, the desire to reassure investors, influence takeover bids, or inflate the value of assets in a particular portfolio at a specific time. The defendants in *Rigby and Bailey* [2005] EWCA Crim 3487, [2006] 2 Cr App R 36 (discussed below) were apparently driven to make false or misleading statements by their firm's impending failure and a desire to avoid a run on its shares. Similarly, a group of senior bankers at Kaupthing were tried in Iceland for involvement in a scheme aimed at boosting public confidence during the financial crisis of 2008. They had, according to media reports, created a misleading demand for Kaupthing shares by secretly lending a major Qatari investor money from the bank itself to buy a tranche of its own shares, but shortly after, the bank collapsed.[1]

Plainly, there can be serious and detrimental consequences of such conduct for individuals, businesses, the economy and society more broadly—hence the reason for its proscription. A crucial question, then, is how precisely market manipulation occurs.

The Main Forms of Manipulation

In 2018, the Fixed Income, Currencies and Commodities (FICC) Market Standards Board (FMSB)[2] compiled a database of over 400 cases of manipulation. Those cases stretched back over 200 years, covering 26 countries and multiple asset classes. The object of the database and its analysis was to understand the root causes of such misconduct. There was much commonality and repetition over time, such that the FSMB found all cases to fall within one of 26 identifiable categories or permutations.[3]

Speaking in broader terms, however, market manipulation is usually committed in one of two ways. The first is by spreading misinformation about a company's prospects to others who are active in the relevant market. For example, a dealer might fraudulently try to persuade another that the current price of a security does not reflect its true value. This can be referred to as 'information-based manipulation'. The second means is giving the relevant market a mistaken impression as to the value of specific financial instruments via misleading conduct, such as the carefully timed use of bids and deals. This is sometimes termed 'transaction-based manipulation'. Sometimes, both of these stratagems are combined.

By way of example, in a 'bear raid', stock market traders may attempt artificially to force down the price of a share, allowing it to be bought back later at a lower price. The traders will then make a profit on a short position (see below) or price rise. A bear raid can be brought about by spreading false but damaging rumours about the target company which then puts

<hr/>

[1] 'Iceland Jails Former Kaupthing Bank Bosses', *BBC News*, 12 December 2013; https://www.bbc.co.uk/news/business-25349240

[2] That is, the body that oversees standards in fixed income, currency and commodity trading.

[3] See generally FICC Market Standards Board, *Behavioural Cluster Analysis; Misconduct in Financial Markets* (2018); https://fmsb.com/wp-content/uploads/2018/07/BCA_v32_1.pdf

downward pressure on the share price. Alternatively, or at the same time, traders might take out a large number of short positions in the company, using these transactions to manipulate the price downwards via the large volume of selling involved. As a result of the misinformation and misleading impressions, other investors may think that the fall in price indicates that there is in fact cause for concern about the target company's profitability and follow suit, pushing the price down even more. This may even trigger further sales from stop loss orders (an order placed with a broker to sell when the equity drops to a certain price, so limiting an investor's loss on a position). The original traders behind the scheme then buy shares back at a lower price to 'cover' their short positions and make a profit.

A few of the more common forms of market manipulation have acquired their own names (some used more frequently in the USA than in the UK). The first two discussed below—'pump and dump' and 'trash and cash' schemes—come under the heading of making misleading statements, or 'information-based' manipulation. The latter three—'wash trading', 'marking the close', and 'spoofing'—might be described as involving misleading conduct, or as 'transaction-based' manipulation.

Pump and Dump

Under pump and dump schemes, a person will acquire a financial instrument, such as a specific equity, then artificially inflate its value through fraudulent promotion. The person will then suddenly sell their holding to unsuspecting parties at the inflated price. As investors come to appreciate that the stock is overvalued, it will rapidly fall back to its original position. In the UK, the 'pumping' phase is sometimes termed 'ramping'. Essentially, a pump and dump scheme creates a form of 'bubble'—except that, unlike ordinary bubbles, it is deliberately and improperly engineered, rather than created spontaneously by market psychology. Such schemes can be traced back to at least the early 1700s, when rumours spread in London's Exchange Alley by existing shareholders artificially inflated the price of the South Sea Company's shares. The shareholders intended to offload their holdings at a profit, but in so doing, also caused one of the earliest stock market crashes.[4]

These schemes come in different forms, ranging from the very complex to the extremely simple. Pump and dump frauds do not necessarily require extensive financial skill to succeed.[5] In a very basic example, from 2000, a 15-year-old high-school student in America used the Internet to promote penny-shares in small companies in which he had already invested. He did this by posting hundreds of messages on Yahoo Finance message boards, using a variety of fictitious names. The messages would claim, *inter alia*, that the companies were making 'tremendous profits' and working on a 'huge number' of deals, so that the shares were currently 'dirt-cheap'. Shares in the small companies briefly soared, allowing him to sell at a substantial profit. The youth eventually reached a mutually-agreed regulatory settlement with the SEC, once his trading activities came to its attention and were investigated.[6]

Another modern, but simple, method of 'pumping' securities involves sending out numerous spam emails to random recipients. For example, one such email, discussing a very thinly traded penny stock in an American oil and gas company, read: 'INVESTOR ALERT! DON'T MISS ANOTHER RUN ON [the company]!!! SOMEBODY KNOWS SOMETHING!!' The stock was priced at $0.0025 and the email predicted it would reach $0.005 by the close of trading. It reached $0.006 but then fell to $0.003 by the end of the day. Although a slight increase on the day, the spread on the stock made it impossible for anyone that purchased and held the share in response to the email to make a profit, and most made a heavy loss.[7]

An apparent case of market manipulation from March 2015 was slightly more sophisticated in form, albeit netting very much more modest returns. The US SEC charged a 37-year-old Bulgarian man for allegedly submitting fictitious takeover bids via the SEC's electronic filing system. The bid used

---

4   Jerry Markham, *Law Enforcement and the History of Financial Market Manipulation* (2014) at 257.

5   Bianca Petcu, 'Fake News and Financial Markets: A 21st Century Twist on Market Manipulation', (2018) 7 *American University Business Law Review* 297 at 301.

6   Gretchen Morgenson, 'SEC Says Teenager Had After-School Hobby: Online Stock Fraud', 21 September 2000, *The New York Times*.

7   Michael Clarke, 'Avoid the Pump and Dump', *This is Money*, 1 September 2006; https://www.thisismoney.co.uk/money/investing/article-1601991/Avoid-the-pump-and-dump.html

fake tender offers and news releases from previously unknown investment firms, issued via an internet-provider in London, to help perpetrate the scheme. The shares briefly increased by 20% before the 'offer' was discounted almost immediately by Avon as bogus. They swiftly fell back when it became obvious that the filing was merely aimed at creating a spike in the company's share price. The perpetrator allegedly held modest positions tied to these equities, which, it was claimed, he sold and made a small profit.[8] The man was arrested in Bulgaria in 2016 but he vehemently denied any wrongdoing and could not be extradited for medical reasons.[9]

Similarly, in July 2015, Twitter's shares jumped more than 8% in just eight minutes after a fake online story began to circulate saying the company had received a $31bn take-over offer. The story mimicked the appearance of a genuine Bloomberg news article with considerable accuracy and carried the byline of one of the news agency's writers. However, after a Bloomberg spokesman tweeted that the report was false, the shares fell back to where they had been within six minutes.[10]

In the UK, the 'City Slickers' trial of 2005 provides another example of a 'pump and dump' scheme. The case involved two financial journalists and their private investor friend. The journalists were employed by *The Daily Mirror* to write a regular column entitled 'City Slickers' which reported news and rumours that affected the value of various shares. Recommendations would be made to readers on the basis of this information. Many readers bought and sold shares on the strength of these recommendations, so that a positive tip, especially the 'Tip of the Day', would normally result in the share price rising significantly. Inevitably, the journalists became aware of this. All three were accused of having made thousands of pounds over six

---

8   Matthew Goldstein, 'SEC Charges Man in Bulgaria in Fake Takeover Offer for Avon', *New York Times*, 4 June 2015; https://www.nytimes.com/2015/06/05/business/dealbook/sec-charges-bulgarian-man-in-fake-takeover-offer-for-avon.html

9   Mariya Chereshева, 'Bulgarian Court Blocks Alleged Fraudster's Extra-dition', *Balkan Insight*, 15 July 2016; https://balkaninsight.com/2016/07/15/bulgarian-court-denies-extradition-to-suspected-wall-street-fraudster-07-15-2016/

10 Sam Thielman, 'Twitter's Shares Jump after Fake Story on Company's $31bn Takeover Offer' *The Guardian*, 14 July 2015; https://www.theguardian.com/technology/2015/jul/14/twitter-shares-fake-story-bloomberg

months between August 1999 and February 2000 by buying shares, publicly tipping them in the newspaper, and then swiftly selling them at a significant profit.[11] All three were convicted or pleaded guilty to conspiracy to contravene section 47(2) of the Financial Services Act 1986 (now replaced by section 89 FSA 2012) by creating a misleading impression as to the value of certain investments.

More generally, Geraint Anderson, a former City trader, has suggested from his personal observation that spreading false rumours by contacting and reporting them to other people in the finance industry was still rife amongst some of his colleagues during the early 2000s. In these situations, hedge fund managers might ring up finance professionals and claim to have heard rumours of a takeover bid for a certain company by (for example) a large American private equity fund, willing to pay a 30% premium to the then share price, and ask if they knew anything about it, while also accepting that it might be total nonsense. They would do this on several occasions, with different professionals, and the financial press might get wind of the rumour and publish it. Perpetrators might even get associates involved, to help spread the rumour, on the basis that 'once it's up four or five per cent, let's get out'. Quite frequently, the shares involved would move up a significant degree, before falling back as positions were closed. It was almost impossible to identify who had originally set the rumour in motion, making any form of action, whether regulatory or criminal, extremely difficult.[12] Because such hedge fund managers could also 'short-stock', they might also profit by resorting to negative rumours and 'trash and cash'.

Trash and Cash

In essence, 'trash and cash' is the inverse of 'pump and dump'. It is also sometimes known as 'stock bashing'. In this situation, an individual attempts to devalue a share by spreading false or exaggerated claims that have a negative impact on the issuing company ('trashing'). After its share price has then dropped, the 'basher' takes a position in it at a lower price than its

---

11   Paul Murphy, 'A Tale of Two City Slickers', *The Guardian*, 12 December 2005; https://www.theguardian.com/money/2005/dec/12/mirror.mondaymediasection

12   Geraint Anderson, *Cityboy: Beer and Loathing in the Square Mile* (Headline, 2008) at 234–237.

true value, hoping to see it increase as the bad news fails to materialise, or is discounted and the share price rights itself.

Trashing can also be used to make money directly from a falling stock price by 'shorting' the shares involved. This is sometimes referred to as 'short and distort', a criminal form of short selling. Short selling works by traders 'borrowing' shares from specialist shareholders who are willing to lend them out for a fee. Until the shares are returned, the borrowers are free to do what they wish with them and do not have to show that they retained possession of them throughout the lending period. The borrowers then sell the shares on to other investors at the (then) market price, in the hope that the share price will subsequently fall. The short seller can then buy them back at a reduced price, before returning them to the original lender, pocketing the difference and making a profit.[13] As a result, short sellers actively desire a fall in the price of a targeted share, and ideally a full-blown collapse in its value. However, if they engineer this artificially, whether by releasing false information or by committing deliberately misleading conduct, they can become market manipulators. It should be noted in this context that the use of contracts for difference (CFDs) also allows a profit to be made on a falling price, and are more readily accessible to smaller scale traders.

In the modern era 'trashing' (like 'pumping') is often conducted by posting misinformation online. For example, in 2000, an American college student created and disseminated a false press release through an online news service for which he had previously worked. The story gave details about an SEC investigation into computer technology company Emulex and the resignation of its CEO, neither of which had in fact occurred. The news was released very shortly before the New York stock market opened and occasioned a temporary fall of 50 percent in the company's share price during the first hour of trading. The student made around US$240,000 in profit, both from short positions and from buying the company's shares before their price rebounded. However, he was subsequently required to

---

13   James Clunie, 'Merchants of Doom', *The Spectator*, 3 March 2018; https://life.spectator.co.uk/articles/merchants-of-doom/

repay investors' losses and a further fine.[14]

In October 2018, in the UK, FTSE 250 company Babcock International Group PLC was the subject of a bleak online report about its prospects by an anonymous/pseudonymous 'research' institute. The story suggested, *inter alia*, that there were problems in the company's relationships with the Ministry of Defence, with whom it had significant contracts. The report is alleged to have caused a 4% fall in the company's share price, wiping £130m off its value in a single day. One leading shareholder suggested that it was a 'blatant piece of market manipulation', while some analysts also suspect short sellers were at work.[15] The following year Babcock was awarded a major contract to build frigates by the MOD.

Wash Trading

Wash trading involves a manipulative trader deliberately selling and repurchasing large quantities of the same stock and so effectively trading with themselves. Wash trading also takes place where a person places simultaneous orders for the sale and purchase of a security through different brokers, or where several traders act in concert to buy and sell an investment.

A simple illustration can be found in the old Canadian criminal case of *Lampard* [1968] 2 OR 470, where the defendant was charged with 29 counts involving wash sales. It was alleged that on one day, for example, he had placed seven orders to buy 38,000 shares, most of them in one company, at 48.5 cents. However, the shares were purchased through six different brokers. On the same day, he placed four orders to sell 35,000 shares (mostly) in the same company, at an identical price, producing eleven wash sales of 34,500 shares. Some 38,500 shares in this particular company were traded on the Stock Exchange that day, so that his dealing made up about 90%

---

14 Alex Berenson, 'Guilty Plea Is Set in Internet Hoax Case Involving Emulex', *New York Times*, 29 December 2000; https://www.nytimes.com/2000/12/29/business/guilty-plea-is-set-in-internet-hoax-case-involving-emulex.html

15 Alan Tovey, 'Should Investors Take Heed of Mysterious Short-seller's Attack on Babcock?', *The Telegraph*; https://www.telegraph.co.uk/business/2018/10/21/should-investors-take-heed-mysterious-short-sellers-attack-babcock/

of the total.[16]

A more recent domestic regulatory action, dealt with by the FSAu in 2011, involved a Salford businessman who had allegedly caused artificial inflation of the price of shares in Global Brands Licensing PLC (GBL). It was claimed that he orchestrated and controlled the great majority of trading in GBL's shares, disguising his involvement behind trading conducted by third parties. As a result, GBL's share price moved from 2p on 24 March 2010, to a peak of 5.25p on 20 April 2010, to his gain.[17]

Through wash trade schemes, although there is no real change in beneficial ownership, such dealings conducted on a sufficient scale and at the right time create a false impression of the level of active trading in the security involved. This attracts other (legitimate) investors into the market, or gives the impression of trading taking place outside the normal price range of a security, both of which inflate its value.[18] The manipulating party is exposed to no real financial risk, and can close their positions to profit from the change in price.

Wash trading can also be used to drive prices down, to similar effect. It should, however, be distinguished from 'churning', another form of manipulation by conduct. That involves a dealer placing both buy and sell orders for a security at the same price with a view to increasing its apparent trade volume, thereby making it more attractive to other investors and, it is hoped, driving its price up as a result.

Marking the Close

Strictly speaking, 'marking the close' involves deliberately buying or selling investments at the close of a market, with the intention of misleading

---

16   Alan Au, 'Stock Market Manipulation after the Financial Services Act 1986' (1989) 2 *Journal of International Banking Law* 53 at 53.

17   James Ferguson, 'FSA Fines Businessman [X] £1m over Share Price Scam', *Manchester Evening News*, 24 May 2011; https://www.manchestereveningnews.co.uk/business/business-news/fsa-fines-businessman-Name]-861365

18   Au, 'Stock Market Manipulation after the Financial Services Act 1986', at 53; Andrew Haynes, 'Market Abuse, Fraud and Misleading Communications' (2012) 19(3) *Journal of Financial Crime* 234–254.

investors who act on the basis of closing (often overnight) prices.[19] A similar but broader notion is defined in article 12(2)(b) MAR, which refers to 'buying or selling of financial instruments, at the opening or closing of the market, which has or is likely to have the effect of misleading investors acting on the basis of the prices displayed, including the opening or closing prices'. Sometimes, even a comparatively limited number of trades can influence a small market or thinly-traded security, if properly timed.

For example, in October 2010, a Dubai-based private investor arranged for a series of pre-planned trades in Reliance Global Depositary Receipts (GDRs) to be executed in the final seconds of an LSE closing auction. This was found to have been done with the intention of artificially raising their price above a certain level. At the time, the investor held a structured financial product in which the payout depended, in part, on the closing price of this specific security on that particular day. By increasing the closing price for Reliance GDRs, he was able to avoid a loss of $3,103,640 under the financial product's terms. The FSAu subsequently concluded that his actions amounted to market manipulation contrary to section 118(5) FSMA 2000. It therefore imposed a regulatory penalty of $6,517,600 under section 123(1) of the 2000 Act, about a third of which was restitution/disgorgement and two-thirds a fine (the latter part being reduced by 30% for early settlement).[20]

Similar to marking the close are deliberate attempts to manipulate the market by buying or selling around the time that reference prices are set. So, for example, in August 2007, a broker at Sucden Financial 'deliberately manipulated' the LIFFE Robusta coffee futures and options markets by organizing a series of trades in the one-minute window when the options reference price was determined. This moved the market up from $1,745 to $1,752 a tonne. In consequence of this conduct, the FSAu subsequently fined him £100,000 and banned him from working in the finance industry for life.[21]

---

19   PlanetCompliance *The 7 Deadly Sins of Market Abuse: An Introduction to the Market Abuse Regime* (2016); https://www.planetcompliance.com/ebooks/ebook-7-deadly-sins-market-abuse/

20   See Jonathan Russell, 'FSA Fines Private Investor [Y] £6m', *The Telegraph*, 9 November 2011.

21   Harry Wilson, 'Coffee Trader Fined for Market Abuse', *The Telegraph*, 3 June 2010; https://www.telegraph.co.uk/finance/markets/7798538/Coffee-trader-fined-for-market-abuse.html

Spoofing

'Spoofing' occurs where a trader tricks the market into thinking that there is more demand to buy or sell a particular financial product than is truly the case. This can occur by placing orders for a large number of the same product, in which the trader will usually already have a position, with no intention of having the orders filled. Other investors see the large orders waiting to be executed and place their own orders at the same level. This drives up the share price, and allows the seller to dispose of his holding at a higher price than would otherwise be the case.[22] Before others can trade on the prices offered, the trader will immediately cancel the orders, giving the further impression that the shares are highly liquid and that there is a healthy market for them. Meanwhile, the trader also takes advantage of the new price by buying or selling again before a correction sets in.

Spoofing can also operate through orders to sell. As the High Court noted in *FCA v Da Vinci Invest Limited* [2015] EWHC 2401 (Ch) (see below), the term simply refers to the fact that the placing of orders creates a false impression as to the dealer's true trading intentions.

'Layering' — entering large orders on one side of an exchange's electronic order book without genuinely intending their execution — is an important form of spoofing. Such orders are usually placed at prices that are unlikely to attract counterparties, but move the price of the share while the market adjusts to the fact that there has been an apparent shift in its supply and demand. This is then followed by the execution of a (usually much smaller) trade on the opposite side of the order book that takes advantage of, and profits from, that movement. This trade is very quickly followed by a cancellation of the large initial order. This sequence is frequently then repeated, but in reverse, as occurred in *Canada Inc v FCA* [2013] EWCA Civ 1662.

The rise of high-frequency trading (HFT), using complex algorithmic computer programmes, has made this form of manipulation very much easier and more effective. Significantly, the growth of HFT since 2006 has coincided with a major increase in the volume of quote messages, while that of trades that are actually carried out has remained relatively stable.

---

22   Sebastian Mock and Marco Ventoruzzo, *Market Abuse Regulation: Commentary and Annotated Guide* (2017) at 315.

The proportion of cancellations has therefore grown over the past decade, in a manner that might well be indicative of increased market manipulation.

However, there can also be entirely legitimate reasons for such cancellations. For example, a trader might quite properly cancel resting orders as market prices move, to prevent them being executed at a loss. When challenged, alleged spoofers will often claim that they had entirely legitimate reasons for cancelling orders and disproving this can be extremely difficult.[23]

An illustrative example is the 2015 case mentioned above of *Da Vinci Invest*, in which the FSAu/FCA sought an injunction against a UK-registered but Swiss-based company, Da Vinci Invest PTE Ltd, and a related Singapore-based company, Da Vinci Invest Ltd. The companies had allegedly committed market manipulation by means of 'layering' between August 2010 and July 2011. The purported mechanism was to place large orders for certain shares on the LSE's electronic trading platform, with no intention of actually trading, then deleting the orders. This had the effect of artificially moving the share price up and down as the market reacted to perceived changes in supply or demand for the securities. The traders were said then to have taken advantage of the small changes in price and made a profit by repeatedly buying shares when their price had been manipulated downwards and selling them when they had been manipulated upwards, in violation of section 118(5) FSMA.[24]

In a similar, regulatory action in 2013, the FCA concluded that a trader had electronically placed and cancelled large orders in commodity futures (such as those for Brent Crude) on the ICE Futures Europe exchange in the UK that he did not intend to be executed. This activity occurred over a six-week period via HFT between September and October 2011 and was done with the intention of creating a misleading impression as to the weight of buyer or seller interest in the security, thereby manipulating the market contrary to section 118(5) FSMA.[25] In reaching its decision to pursue action against the trader, the FCA noted that his substantial orders were typically resting on the order book for less than one second. The FCA concluded that

---

23   Fisher et al, 'Criminal Forms of High Frequency Trading', at 118.

24   See *FCA v Da Vinci Invest Limited* [2015] EWHC 2401 (Ch).

25   FCA, *Final Notice*, 3 July 2013.

placing them for such a short period of time, and automatically cancelling the remainder of a large order in the event of a partial execution, made it very unlikely that the large orders would be executed: 'However, the false impression of liquidity ... made it more likely that the small order would trade as market participants were induced to trade on the opposite side of the order book to the large layered orders'.[26]

Moving abroad, and to consider a more 'traditional' *modus operandi*, in November 2016 Singaporean authorities alleged that three people had played a major role in the country's largest ever market manipulation case. The conduct itself had led to a crash in three local stocks during the autumn of 2013. It was claimed that the traders' scheme involved over 180 secretly-controlled trading accounts and made thousands of orders for low-worth shares. This produced huge, short-term increases in the shares' value, but the relevant companies then lost $5.6 billion in combined market worth over a few frenzied trading sessions the same October.[27]

Returning to the UK, a former bond trader at Bank of America Merrill Lynch, was fined £60,000 in a 2017 regulatory action. He had engaged in market abuse contrary to section 118(5) FSMA by giving misleading impressions with regard to the price and demand for Dutch state loans in fixed income markets. The bond trader made a €22,000 profit for his employer in the summer of 2014 by taking advantage of algorithmic traders on the BrokerTec electronic trading platform. This occurred on a dozen occasions; on eleven of them he appeared to be a bidder when he was actually a seller, and on one occasion he did the opposite. His approach was designed to induce market participants tracking quotes to raise or lower their quotes to his advantage.[28]

In an increasingly interconnected financial world, the consequences of such abuse can be very serious and widespread. For example, in 2010, a private trader operating from his home in London pleaded guilty to using

---

26   Ibid.

27   Jeevan Vasagar, 'Couple Charged in Singapore Exchange "Penny Stock Crash" Case', *Financial Times*, 25 November 2016; https://www.ft.com/content/543f2686-b2f7-11e6-a37c-f4a01fib0fa1

28   *Financial Times*, 22 November 2017; FCA, *Final Notice*, 22 November 2017; https://www.fca.org.uk/publication/final-notices/Name-2017.pdf

automated trading software to 'spoof' the US stock market by placing and cancelling up to 19,000 orders in under a second. It was claimed that this helped to destabilise markets and contributed to triggering a 'flash crash' that ultimately, if very temporarily, wiped hundreds of billions of dollars from the value of US shares in a matter of minutes.[29]

Intention Is (Often) Everything

As can be seen from some of the above cases, when it comes to conduct-based market manipulation at least, it is not behavior itself but the mental state behind it that makes it unlawful. As Le Blanc J observed in *De Berenger* (1814) 3 M&S 67, 'A man may have occasion to sell out a large sum, which may have the effect of depressing the price of stocks, or may buy in a large sum, and thereby raise the price on a particular day, and yet he will be guilty of no offence'. Allegations of market manipulation often boil down to whether trades were made in good faith or, instead, were done to prompt movements in the market advantageous to the dealer.

For example, consider the 2014 regulatory action in which the FCA fined an experienced bond dealer £662,700 and prohibited him from regulated activity. It was alleged that he had sought to rig the gilts market by buying £331 million of a UK government gilt called UKT 8.75% 2017[30] between 9am and 2.30 pm on 10 October 2011. This bond was relatively illiquid, and his purchases represented approximately 2,700% of its average daily traded total over the previous four months, so that his dealing pushed its price up significantly. These were added to an existing holding of over £500 million in UKT 8.75% 2017.

Vitally, this trading took place on the first day of the second round of quantitative easing in the UK, which had been announced five days earlier. That meant that the Bank of England purchased certain types of gilt, such as UKT 8.75% 2017, with a view to injecting money directly into the economy and stimulating growth. Offers for the sale of eligible gilts could be made to the Bank of England (BoE) in the half hour after 2.15 pm on

---

29   Aruna Viswanatha, '"Flash Crash" [A] Pleads Guilty to Spoofing', *Wall Street Journal*, 10 November 2016.

30   Such bonds are identified by reference to the yearly interest they pay and their maturity date.

10 October 2011. During this period, the dealer offered to sell £850 million of the bond, which included the £331 million he had acquired earlier that same day. The offer price for the bonds to the BoE, which the dealer hoped it would accept, was, of course, based upon its now-increased market price.

The FCA concluded that the bond dealer's intense trading on 10 October was specifically designed to move the price of the bond to an abnormal and artificial level, thereby increasing the profit made from any subsequent sale to the BoE. In the event, the BoE quickly identified the bond's highly unusual price movement and rejected all offers. The dealer then stopped buying, and the gilt's price went into reverse. The regulator concluded that his behaviour amounted to market abuse within the meaning of section 118(5) FSMA because it gave a 'false or misleading impression' as to the demand for UKT 8.75% 2017, with a view to making imminent sales. The regulator also noted that the dealer had had an opportunity to buy the gilt in a more gradual fashion before 10 October, so reducing the impact of his purchase on the market, but had refrained from doing so. This suggested that he was trying to move the market, not simply to acquire more of a bond that he perceived as cheap, as he suggested.

The FCA's case was greatly bolstered by telephone calls relating to transactions and client orders, which had been preserved as required by FSAu/FCA rules since March 2009.[31] The FCA considered these to show the dealer had an intention to 'Get it [the bond] way up' before offering it to the BoE.

This case was the FCA's first successful regulatory action for manipulation of the gilt market, but it is unlikely to be the last.

---

31   See FCA, *Handbook* at COBS 11.8.

CHAPTER 3

Identifying and Investigating Market Manipulation

Introduction

When the FSMA came into force in mid-2001, the newly established Financial Services Authority (FSAu) assumed primary responsibility for dealing with market abuse in the UK. The Department of Trade and Industry (which was disbanded in 2007)[1] and the Serious Fraud Office (SFO) also retained some involvement in investigations and prosecutions, especially during the early years of this century.

The Financial Services Act 2012 (FSA 2012) renamed and retasked (with some changes) the FSAu as the Financial Conduct Authority (FCA),[2] which began operating as such on 1 April 2013.[3] The FCA is still the main agency that investigates and prosecutes market manipulation. It is not publicly-funded, but rather is supported by fees charged to the firms that it regulates.[4] In October 2012, the FSAu estimated that this would encompass about 26,000 firms from across the finance industry.[5] However, by December 2017, the FCA calculated that it had authorised and now regulated over 56,000 firms. Very importantly, the FCA also regulates everyone who participates in those markets — not only those trading from within large financial enterprises, but also small-scale, independent financial advisers.[6]

---

1   See 'Department of Trade and Industry'; https://www.gov.uk/government/organisations/
    department-of-trade-and-industry

2   See section 6 FSA 2012 and section 1A FSMA.

3   'About the FCA', *Financial Conduct Authority*, 30 July 2019; https://www.fca.org.uk/about/
    the-fca

4   Ibid.

5   FSAu, *Journey to the FCA* (2012); https://www.fca.org.uk/publication/corporate/fsa-journey-to-
    the-fca.pdf at 25.

6   FCA, *FCA Mission: Our Approach to Authorisation* (2017); https://www.fca.org.uk/publication/
    corporate/our-approach-authorisation.pdf at 6.

This is by virtue of the general prohibition on carrying-on any regulated activity—in general terms, a specified kind of activity carried on by way of business, relating to an investment of a specified kind or to property—unless authorised or exempt.[7]

The FCA has statutory power to prosecute a range of criminal offences, including the conduct of regulated activities without its authorisation, and to enforce the obligations contained in the MAR.[8]

Meanwhile, the SFO has a statutory obligation to investigate and prosecute cases involving serious or complex fraud,[9] which can extend to those involving market abuse but, in light of their broader contexts, are normally seen as outside the FCA's remit. For example, in 2011, it was the SFO that conducted the prosecution of Stuart Pearson for making misleading statements contrary to section 397 FSMA.[10] Similarly, in 2013, the SFO brought criminal charges against Tom Hayes, a former trader at UBS and Citigroup, for conspiracy to defraud at common law by manipulating the London Inter Bank Offered Rate (LIBOR).[11] As discussed below, that did not become a specific statutory offence in its own right until April 2013, when section 91 FSA 2012 came into force. A tranche of LIBOR and EURIBOR trials and retrials (in consequence of 'hung' juries) occurred in 2018 and 2019, all of which were prosecuted by the SFO.[12]

However, prior to the SFO's involvement, the FSAu had extensively investigated the alleged rigging of LIBOR, in the years after the global financial crisis. These investigations resulted in regulatory proceedings against a number of financial institutions for their acquiescence in an excessively relaxed supervisory regime. This culminated in Barclays Bank PLC *inter alia*, admitting its involvement in manipulation, including making US dollar

---

7   Sections 19 and 22 FSMA, and the Financial Services and Markets Act 2000 (Regulated Activities) Order 2001.

8   See section 401 FSMA, sections 1L and 204A FSA 2012, and article 2 of the Financial Services and Markets Act 2000 (Qualifying EU Provisions) Order 2013.

9   See section 1 of the Criminal Justice Act 1987.

10 Julia Kollewe, 'Former Langbar Chief Jailed over Fraud', *The Guardian*, 20 June 2011; https://www.theguardian.com/law/2011/jun/20/former-langbar-chief-jailed-fraud

11 See generally *Hayes* [2015] EWCA Crim 1944, [2018] 1 Cr App R 3.

12 The SFO publishes a list of its cases at https://www.sfo.gov.uk/our-cases/

LIBOR and EURIBOR submissions that took into account requests made by its own interest rate derivatives' traders and even traders at other banks. (The dealers sought to benefit Barclays' trading positions). The FSAu issued Barclays with a fine of £59.5 million under section 206 FSMA 2000 in June 2012.[13] The remit of the SFO and the FCA is, therefore, interconnected to the extent that some observers have suggested their merger. For the time being, however, the FCA is the prime mover in connection with market manipulation, at least where wider issues do not arise.

Detection

In June 2018, Mark Steward, then Director of Enforcement and Market Oversight at the FCA, noted that the ability to detect and investigate suspected misconduct early on needed to improve. Higher fines and other penalties, on their own, would not lead to effective enforcement, 'if we don't have robust, accurate and faithful processes for detecting misconduct in all its guises'.[14]

That is not to say that the FCA is ineffectual. Rather, cases of market manipulation come to the FCA's attention by being reported (including, theoretically, by self-reporting) or through exposure by the FCA's own market monitoring. According to the FCA, information from whistle-blowers may provide the earliest indications of wrongdoing.[15] Indeed, an electronic hotline has been established to communicate with the FCA (whistle@fca.org.uk)[16] and whistleblowing appears to be on the rise: there was a 24% increase in such reports in 2018, with the FCA receiving 1,755 reports as compared to 1,420 the previous year.[17]

13　FSAu, *Final Notice: Barclays Bank PLC*, 27 June 2012; https://www.fca.org.uk/publication/final-notices/barclays-jun12.pdf

14　Mark Steward, 'Has the Industry Improved Ten Years On?' (speech delivered at the Banking Litigation and Regulation Forum, London, 14 June 2018).

15　FCA, *FCA Mission: Our Approach to Enforcement* (2018); https://www.fca.org.uk/publication/corporate/our-approach-enforcement-final-report-feedback-statement.pdf ('FCA—*Approach to Enforcement*') at 9.

16　Whistleblowers can also write to, or telephone, the FCA's Intelligence Department in London: see https://www.fca.org.uk/firms/whistleblowing

17　Caroline Binham, 'Whistleblowing Complaints to UK Regulator Rise 24%', *Financial Times*, 3 March 2019; https://www.ft.com/content/da9eocce-3c52-11e9-b72b-2c7f526ca5do

The FCA has taken an active decision not to pay rewards to whistleblowers at present.[18] This is despite the fact that such payments are permitted by MAR, provided the information is new, leads to action against the infringer, and the whistleblower does not have an existing obligation to report it.[19] Despite the lack of incentives, there is nonetheless a measure of protection for whistleblowers in the UK. Where it applies, the Public Interest Disclosure Act 1998 makes clear that such individuals should not, on that basis, be dismissed or victimised. The MAR also requires that whistleblowing schemes afford appropriate protection.

For these reasons, in 2018, the FCA and the Prudential Regulation Authority (PRA) jointly fined the chief executive officer of Barclays Group £642,430. He had tried to identify the author of an anonymous letter expressing allegations, including some made against the CEO himself. In so doing, he failed to realise his own conflict of interest and interfered with the proper internal systems for addressing whistleblowers' concerns.[20] The FCA's executive director of enforcement and market oversight observed that: 'Whistleblowers play a vital role in exposing poor practice and misconduct in the financial services sector. It is critical that individuals are able to speak up anonymously and without fear of retaliation if they want to raise concerns.'[21]

Nevertheless, those who are authorised and regulated by the FCA supply far more information on manipulation than do whistleblowers, as a result of statutory and regulatory obligations. For instance, article 16(2) MAR, which deals with the prevention and detection of market abuse, requires market operators and investment firms who run trading venues to establish and maintain effective arrangements, systems, and procedures for detecting market manipulation. These must be proportionate to the size and nature of their business activity, taking into account the nature of their typical clients and employees, the financial instruments traded and the services

---

18   See FCA and Bank of England Prudential Authority, *Financial Incentives for Whistleblowers* (2014); https://www.fca.org.uk/publication/financial-incentives-for-whistleblowers.pdf and FCA—*Approach to Enforcement*, at 20.

19   See recital 74.

20   FCA, 'FCA and PRA Jointly Fine [B] £642,430 and Announce Special Requirements Regarding Whistleblowing Systems and Controls at Barclays', 11 May 2018.

21   Ibid.

they provide.[22]

In most cases, a fully-automated system will be necessary to satisfy this requirement, one that has a complex event processing (CEP) capacity that is able to analyse large amounts of information from multiple sources and which can 'red flag' suspicious transactions. The European Securities and Markets Authority (ESMA) has emphasised the importance of such automated monitoring systems being able to evaluate transactions both individually and in the context of other orders. However, there must also be an appropriate level of human analysis in the monitoring of potential market manipulation. Relevant documentation must be preserved for at least five years, including the reasons for submitting or, even more importantly, not submitting a suspicious transaction and order report (see below) when an apparently suspicious transaction is flagged-up. This must be made available to the FCA on request.

As a result, although market professionals will sometimes personally observe strange or 'out of character' deals or behaviour amongst their clients, such as repeat orders and cancellations that are not in keeping with their usual trading behaviour and strategies, they will often be alerted to manipulation by in-house electronic surveillance. For example, in *Da Vinci Invest*, a bank that provided the custodian services necessary to facilitate the dealing of a group of traders terminated its agreement with them after its own surveillance systems identified several occasions on which the traders, operating through one of the companies involved, bought a particular security at the bottom of a periodic price variation and sold it at its top. The bank then filed a suspicious transaction report (STR) to the FCA identifying the company as being potentially responsible for market abuse contrary to section 118 FSMA.

A failure by companies to maintain proper surveillance can lead to severe consequences, even if no manipulation occurs. In 2019, the FCA fined Linear Investments Limited £409,300 pursuant to section 206 FSMA, for failing to provide adequate risk management and electronic surveillance systems for the detection of market abuse between January 2013 and August 2015.

---

22   See article 2 of the Commission Delegated Regulation 2016/957.

That decision was later upheld by the UT(TCC).[23] The company had been slow to realise that post-trade surveillance undertaken by brokers was not enough to discharge its regulatory obligations. It had subsequently installed an automated post-trade surveillance system, although this took time to operate effectively, and there had been further periods during which Linear had had to disable alerts on the automated system in relation to spoofing and insider dealing because it had not been properly calibrated. There was inadequate surveillance during these periods. It was not claimed that any market abuse had actually occurred, and there had been no impropriety by the company, but this may be seen as a cautionary tale in favour of compliance with monitoring obligations.

Similarly, in January 2018, the FCA fined Interactive Brokers (UK) (IBUK) £1,049,412 for failings in its systems for identifying and reporting suspicious transactions in 2014–2015. IBUK, a London based online broker, arranged and executed transactions in certain financial instruments, including CFDs, directly for its UK clients, and also executed trades on behalf of other members of Interactive Brokers Group (IBG). The company delegated its post-trade monitoring to a team within IBG based in the US. However, IBUK failed properly to design or calibrate the monitoring system used, or to test its operation so as to ensure that potential market abuse by its clients would be identified. Nor did it provide effective oversight of the US team's reviews of the reports it produced or adequate training for the staff conducting these reviews. This heightened the risk of IBUK failing to submit appropriate STRs to the FCA. IBUK's systems 'fell below the appropriate standards and exposed counterparties and the market to risks they did not bargain for'.[24]

In practice, the combined input of both experienced staff and automated surveillance are often crucial, and work together, the former being used to assess alerts generated by the latter.

Once a suspicious transaction that suggests possible market manipulation

---

23 See *Linear Investments Limited v FCA* [2019] UKUT 0115 (TCC).

24 See FCA, 'FCA Fines Interactive Brokers (UK) Limited £1,049,412 for Poor Market Abuse Controls and Failure to Report Suspicious Client Transactions', 25 January 2018; https://www.fca.org.uk/news/press-releases/fca-fines-interactive-brokers-uk-limited

has come to light, it must be reported via a STOR to the FCA.

STORs[25]

Pursuant to article 16(2) MAR, persons professionally arranging or executing transactions regulated thereunder are required to report to the FCA any transaction or order that they have reasonable grounds to suspect might constitute actual or attempted market manipulation. The MAR is supplemented in this respect by Commission Delegated Regulation 2016/957, which provides a template for how those reports should be made, namely in the form of a STOR. (These were previously simply STRs, but in 2016, reporting requirements were extended by MAR to cover 'orders' as well as completed transactions.)

For example, a STOR might be filed regarding an order for shares that is cancelled, but which a dealer suspects was intended to be manipulative. A STOR would also have to be submitted even if a broker has refused to place a particular order for a customer. It should be noted that the obligation to submit a STOR also applies to suspicious transactions that occur in the context of over the counter (OTC) trading in derivatives, where the underlying instrument is itself traded on a regulated market.

The threshold for reporting a potential case of market manipulation to the FCA via a STOR is relatively low. It is merely necessary that there should be sufficient indications that the relevant transaction or order *could* constitute market abuse. However, as the regulator has noted, sometimes this will not become apparent until after the transaction has taken place, while some abusive orders will only appear suspicious when seen in relation to other transactions or conduct, at which point the obligation to report will become operative.[26] Once reasonable suspicion has formed, a STOR should be submitted 'without delay' and any failure to do so can be penalised by the FCA. Even so, the FCA considers that there has been little recent evidence of defensive reporting of transactions that fail to meet the reasonable suspicion threshold.

---

25 For more extensive commentary on the STOR process, see Anderson et al, *A Practitioner's Guide*, at 1.8.1.

26 FCA *Handbook* at SUP 15.10.

The report should be made using an FCA approved template, and following guidance set out by the regulator in June 2016.[27] It should provide as much information as possible, so that the validity of the suspicion can be assessed reasonably quickly, and an investigation initiated if deemed appropriate. In particular, it should contain the identity of the person submitting the STOR; the capacity in which they operate (for example, as a broker); a description of the relevant transaction; why the reporter suspects that it might constitute actual or attempted market manipulation; the means of identifying any person involved in the suspicious order or transaction; and any other information and supporting documents which may be relevant.[28] The reporter should never inform the subject of the STOR that it has submitted, as this might compromise any investigation.

There has been a general upward trend in the number of STRs/STORs submitted over recent years as traders have become more aware of their obligations and the dangers of failing to fulfil them, something that has been reinforced by the advent of MAR. A record 3,730 STORs relating to suspected insider dealing and market manipulation (mainly the former) were submitted to the FCA in the first nine months of 2017, which was 24% more than in all of 2016 when the figure stood at 3,008.[29] In 2018, the figure for the entire year reached 5,926.[30] The great majority of STORs involved equities, rather than commodities, fixed income securities (bonds), or FX (foreign exchange sometimes called 'forex') transactions. The FCA's director of market oversight has suggested that firms could improve their reporting

---

27   Ibid.

28   See FCA, *Guide to Submitting a Suspicious Transaction and Order Report (STOR) Using Connect* (2018); https://www.fca.org.uk/publication/systems-information/suspicious-transaction-order-report-stor-connect-guide.pdf

29   FCA, 'Number of STORs Received: 2017', 13 February 2019 https://www.fca.org.uk/markets/suspicious-transaction-and-order-reports/number-stors-received-2017; FCA, 'Number of STORs Received: 3 July-31 December 2016', 13 February 2019 https://www.fca.org.uk/markets/suspicious-transaction-and-order-reports/number-stors-received-3-july-31-december-2016; FCA, 'Number of STORs Received: 2007-2 July 2016', 13 February 2019 https://www.fca.org.uk/markets/suspicious-transaction-and-order-reports/number-strs-received-2007-2-july-2016

30   FCA, 'Number of STORs Received: 2018', 13 February 2019 https://www.fca.org.uk/markets/suspicious-transaction-and-order-reports/number-stors-received-2018

in these areas, particularly in respect of fixed income transactions.[31]

However, the FCA also conducts its own surveillance of various markets using its new Market Data Processor (MDP). The MDP system receives and inputs a huge quantity of data pursuant to MiFID II from the UK financial industry and some non-UK EEA financial market participants. These range from transaction reports to those relating to commodity derivatives positions.[32] At its simplest, this should identify a previously 'flat lining' share that suddenly surges without any obvious explanation, such as a takeover bid. The increasing use of sophisticated algorithms and complex event processing to analyse the large amount of information available should help to facilitate the exposure of manipulation.

Investigations

Once possible market manipulation comes to the attention of the FCA's Enforcement and Market Oversight Division (EMOD or 'Enforcement'), it will have to make a decision on whether formally to pursue the matter and appoint specialist investigators pursuant to s168 FSMA. Only a small proportion of apparently suspicious activity that comes to the regulator's notice is the subject of formal investigation. In many cases, action is not taken after initial scrutiny.[33]

For example, EMOD's Annual Performance Report for the year 2016–2017 indicates that only 29 investigations into possible market manipulation were started, while just 78 were opened for insider dealing, despite the many hundreds of STORS having been received and the FCA's own active surveillance of the markets. In the year from April 2017 to April 2018, the FCA opened 19 investigations into market manipulation and closed 13.[34] More recently, in response to a freedom of information request, the FCA confirmed that it had only opened 61 investigations into insider dealing

---

31 Hoggett, 'Effective Compliance'.

32 See FCA, 'Market Data Reporting and MDP'; https://www.fca.org.uk/markets/market-data-regimes/market-data-reporting-mdp

33 Paul Barnes, 'Insider Dealing and Market Abuse: The UK's Record on Enforcement' (2011) 39 *International Journal of Law, Crime and Justice* 174–189 at 187.

34 FCA, *Enforcement Annual Performance Report 2017/18* (2018); https://www.fca.org.uk/publication/corporate/annual-report-2017-18-enforcement-performance.pdf at 6.

(not market manipulation) in the eleven months from April 2018, although it received over 5,000 STORs for the same form of market abuse in 2018.

Even with the small number of investigations opened, the FCA has stressed that this does not necessarily mean it is persuaded at the outset that misconduct has occurred, merely that it wishes to gain a full understanding of the facts.[35] The FCA is keener than previously to use investigations as a diagnostic tool, rather than merely employing them where the evidence is very strongly suggestive of wrongdoing. Very occasionally, the potential subject of an investigation may be approached for information before such a decision.[36] Sometimes, very minor technical, breaches that might constitute market abuse might be dealt with informally.[37]

It should be noted that the process of requiring STORS to be submitted in market abuse cases has some enforcement benefits, irrespective of whether they prompt investigations. In 2019, the FCA's director of enforcement observed that since the regulator began engaging more overtly with abuse, there had been a decrease in the number of STORs filed by certain firms. This was apparently because they had 'off-boarded' some of their clients who were repeatedly behaving suspiciously.[38] Alternatively, and less drastically, a firm might mitigate future risks of manipulation by restricting the access of such clients to particular markets or financial instruments, or by setting pre-trade limits on their potential dealings. They can also conduct enhanced monitoring of those clients whose behaviour has been identified as potentially suspicious on earlier occasions.

Where the FCA appoints investigators to look into a person's activities, it is not obliged to notify that person if there are circumstances suggesting that they have committed an offence under sections 89–91 FSA 2012, or a breach of article 15.[39] Nonetheless, FCA policy is normally to give notice to

---

35   See FCA 'Investigation Opening Criteria', 24 April 2019 https://www.fca.org.uk/about/enforcement/investigation-opening-criteria

36   Clare McMullen and Elly Proudlock, 'United Kingdom: Financial Services Enforcement and Investigation', in Marieke Breijer (ed), *The European, Middle Eastern and African Investigations Review 2018* (2018, Global Investigations Review) 56–60 at 52–59.

37   See FCA, *Handbook* at EG 2.1.4.

38   Hoggett, 'Dynamic Response'.

39   Sections 168(2) and 170 FSMA.

a person under such investigation 'when it exercises its statutory powers to require information from them, providing such notification will not, in the FCA's view, prejudice the FCA's ability to conduct the investigation effectively'.[40] Once this has occurred, an investigative interview will often follow fairly swiftly, whether after arrest or by pre-arranged appointment,. Arrest might be sought (on the basis of existing police powers of arrest) where, for example, it appears likely that inviting an individual to attend an interview on a voluntary basis might prejudice the investigation, risk destruction of evidence, or allow the dissipation of assets.[41]

The FCA can in certain circumstances also apply to a magistrates' court for a search warrant that allows a constable (who may be accompanied by an FCA investigator if so authorised) to enter premises in order to look for evidence.[42] More generally, recordings of telephone conversations and data traffic records from financial firms and institutions, documenting the execution of transactions, along with records from telecommunications operators, will be recovered. These often constitute crucial evidence in the detection of market abuse, for example by establishing who is responsible for the dissemination of misleading information or that a relationship exists between certain people.[43] Statements will of course also be taken from potential witnesses.

The Investigative Interview

The investigative interview, with questioning carried out by FCA officers, is an important stage in both criminal prosecutions and regulatory actions for market manipulation. The substantial overlap between the two means that both are usually possibilities when suspected manipulation first comes to light. Nonetheless, it is only when an individual is specifically suspected of a criminal offence that an interview will be conducted under caution with all the safeguards contained in the Police and Criminal Evidence Act

---

40   See FCA, *Handbook* at EG 4.2.2; see also EG 4.3.1.

41   Ibid at EG 4.2.4.

42   Section 176 FSMA.

43   Recital 65 MAR.

1984 and its attendant Codes of Practice (particularly Codes C, E and F).[44]

Even when they follow an arrest, answering questions in such interviews is voluntary for the accused, as compared with interviews conducted by the FCA pursuant to its statutory powers to require an individual to attend and answer questions or provide documents. However, what is said during PACE-compliant interviews in respect of criminal offences is admissible in evidence against the accused; what is said during compulsory statutory interviews is not, although an individual may be prosecuted for failure attend for, or do as required in, such an interview.[45] It is FCA practice generally to split the interview into sections of 45 minutes to an hour, with ten- to 15-minute breaks between each section.[46]

For most suspects in market manipulation cases, having a suitably experienced solicitor present is particularly important, not least to advise on whether to answer the investigators' questions. For specific discussion of the caution and adverse inferences from silence, reference should be had to core practitioner texts.[47] Nonetheless, it bears noting that, in cases of market manipulation, there may well be good reason not to draw an adverse inference from a person's failure to answer questions: the complexity of the material and the circumstances around it may mean that no sensible response is immediately feasible: *Roble* [1997] EWCA Crim 118. Moreover, in 2005, the Lord Chief Justice issued a protocol regarding control and management of heavy fraud and other complex criminal cases, in which it was observed that many interviews in such cases were too long and unstructured. It was urged therefore that interviews be used to enable suspects to respond to the allegations against them, rather than to discuss every document in the case.[48]

At the conclusion of the initial interview, if there is sufficient evidence, a suspect may be charged and remanded in custody or on police bail.

---

44   FCA, *Handbook* at EG 4.2.1.

45   Ibid at EG 4.8.

46   Claire Cross, 'FCA Enforcement Interviews: Tips and Best Practice', 25 September 2017; http://www.corkerbinning.com/fca-enforcement-interviews-tips-and-best-practice/#page=1

47   See *Blackstone's Criminal Practice* (2019, OUP) at Section F20; *Archbold Criminal Pleading and Practice* (2019, Sweet & Maxwell) at Chapter 15, Part II.

48   See http://www.justice.gov.uk/courts/procedure-rules/criminal/pd-protocol/pd_protocol

Alternatively, they can be released under investigation[49] or on bail without charge, and further interviews may be held. This may be necessary in light of the initial questioning, or after other investigations, such as examination of seized documents, have been carried out. This can be a lengthy process. Nevertheless, the FCA will at some point have to decide how to proceed: it may conclude that there is no basis for any action to be taken; that very minor or technical examples of manipulative activity can be addressed without the need for any type of enforcement action; or, given the gravity of the conduct, that it is necessary to pursue regulatory proceedings or even criminal prosecution.[50]

Criminal Prosecution or Regulatory Action?

It has been observed that, in market abuse investigations, there is a continuum of behaviour ranging 'from deliberate criminal wrong-doing, to regulatory wrong-doing, to errors of judgement that might not meet the definition of serious misconduct'.[51] Unfortunately, there is no neat legal distinction between the first two categories; rather, there is very substantial overlap between articles 15 and 12 MAR, and the criminal offences in Part 7 FSA 2012. In the past it has even been suggested that, technically, almost any activity that amounted to market abuse for the purposes of a regulatory action under section 118 FSMA (which was replaced by MAR) would also have been a criminal offence, whether under the Fraud Act 2006, at common law, or under section 397 FSMA (now replaced by the Part 7 FSA 2012 offences).[52]

Nonetheless, the overlap is not complete; MAR and the FSA 2012 are further apart than were the prior regimes. Even then, there were important definitional differences between regulatory and criminal actions. For

---

49   This is a mechanism introduced under section 52 of the Policing and Crime Act 2017, amending PACE section 30A dealing with bail without charge. Release under investigation means that a person is released unconditionally after being arrested or taken into custody, while authorities continue their inquiries. Unlike bail, there is no time limit on how long a person may remain under investigation and no requirement for a court periodically to review the position.

50   FCA, *Approach to Enforcement*, at 10.

51   Hoggett, 'Dynamic Response'.

52   Haynes, 'Market Abuse, Fraud and Misleading Communications' at 234–254.

example, in the case involving Canada Inc, it appears that the FCA opted to bring regulatory rather than criminal proceedings primarily because the former did not require proof of inducement. Instead, it was only necessary (and possible) to show that a regular user of the market would regard the behaviour as falling short of reasonable expectations of acceptable market practice.[53]

More generally, what has been termed 'classic' market manipulation usually involves the making of misleading statements or impressions to the market that are, in many ways, akin to fraud. Such conduct is therefore morally culpable, something that has been reflected in the criminal offences that govern the field, which normally require proof of at least recklessness, if not manipulative intent. However, under MAR, the concept of 'market manipulation' has been expanded to encompass not just deliberately or recklessly misleading the market but also doing so regardless of mental state in situations where that outcome is merely likely.

For example, article 12(1)(a)(i) MAR prohibits orders or transactions that give, or are likely to give, 'false or misleading signals' as to the supply or demand for a security, *unless* the person involved establishes that their behaviour was for 'legitimate reasons' and conforms with accepted market practices, as established by a competent authority in accordance with article 13 (and there are very few of these). Thus, if distorting conduct alone is proven, it then falls for the trader to rebut this by establishing that it was carried out in that exculpatory manner (see *Chapter 5* of this work). Similarly, under article 12(1)(c) and article 12(1)(d), disseminating or transmitting misleading information through the media, or in relation to a financial benchmark, is a regulatory offence where the defendant 'knew or ought to have known' that it was false or misleading. An individual's mental state is central to their culpability; the fact that the MAR requires no or lesser mental elements indicates their lower seriousness and hence the lesser punishments available.

For illustration, suppose that a trader is holding a large tranche of shares in XYZ PLC, a very thinly traded penny share. He has a hunch that the

---

53   Fisher et al, 'Criminal Forms of High Frequency Trading', at 117.

share is very good value but is also concerned that it is a potentially risky investment. In the last hour of the trading day, he makes an offer for a large number of further shares in the company. Before the order is fulfilled, he gets cold feet and cancels it. He does this a second time. He finally makes a purchase of the shares, just before the market closes. The combined effect of this activity is to drive up the closing price of the stock. This continues to rise in the first few minutes of the following day's trading, as the overnight price continues to influence the market, at which point the trader, noticing that he is sitting on a modest profit, once again gets cold feet and decides to close his position, selling his shares in the company. He would not have committed an offence under section 90 FSA 2012, because he did not 'intend' to create any impression (see below). However, he *might* fall foul of article 12(1)(a)(i) MAR, if he could not persuade the court that he traded for legitimate reasons and in conformity with an accepted market practice.

Nevertheless, with these caveats, in most cases, criminal and regulatory actions will both be potential options on the same set of facts. To take a simple illustration, consider the trader who purchases a large quantity of shares in a certain company. He then starts leaving messages in various internet investment chatrooms claiming untruthfully that the company has secured a huge order, one that will transform its fortunes; the shares increase in value by 15% and he closes his position, making a small profit. This might well constitute an offence under section 89(1)(a) FSA 2012, as he is making a statement which he knows to be false or misleading in a material respect and his statements are at least reckless as to how others might respond to that (see *Chapter 3*). However, it would also constitute a violation of article 12(1)(c) MAR, as it entails disseminating information through the internet which gives, or is likely to give, false or misleading signals as to the supply of, demand for, or price of, a financial instrument (see *Chapter 5*). As a result, both options of criminal prosecution and regulatory action would be open to the FCA when considering the matter.

The FCA has stated firmly that if it investigates market abuse that might be the subject of criminal or regulatory proceedings, it will not decide straightaway which route to follow. It will wait to make sure that there is a proper understanding of the case before this decision is made.[54]

One of the reasons why this decision is a difficult one is that it presents a clear fork in the road, from which there can be no return. The principle of double jeopardy would seem to mean that regulatory proceedings may not be brought where a criminal prosecution has been unsuccessful (or vice versa).[55] Although this has not been definitively ruled upon by a British court, there is support for the FCA's position. First, other EU countries with bifurcated systems have reached the same conclusion in this regard. For example, the French *Code Monétaire et Financier* was amended to prevent actions for market abuse under both criminal and regulatory law, following a 2015 ruling by the French Constitutional Court that this violated the equivalent Roman law principle against double punishment. As such, if the *Autorité des Marchés Financiers* pursues a market abuse case, the criminal prosecutor is now barred from doing so, and vice versa.[56]

Secondly, in March 2018, the FCA's interpretation received partial support from the Court of Justice of the European Union in its decision in *Garlsson Real Estate v Commissione Nazionale Per Le Società E La Borsa (Consob)* [2018] Lloyd's Rep FC 288. In that case, the court considered article 4 of Protocol 7 to the European Convention of Human Rights (ECHR), and article 50 of the Charter of Fundamental Rights of the European Union.[57] Both articles provide in substantially the same terms that no-one shall be liable to be tried or punished again in criminal proceedings for an offence for which they have already been finally acquitted or convicted according to law. Under the terms of the charter, that protection applies to proceedings that may occur in any EU Member State, while the ECHR expressly refers only to proceedings within the same state.

---

54 FCA—*Approach to Enforcement*, at 11.

55 FCA, *Handbook* at EG 12.10.

56 See *Autorité des Marchés Financiers*, 'A New System for the Punishment of Market Abuse in France', 2 December 2016; https://www.amf-france.org/en_US/Reglementation/Dossiers-thematiques/l-AMF/Fonctionnement-de-l-AMF-et-reformes-du-secteur-financier/Un-nouveau-systeme-pour-la-repression-des-abus-de-marche-en-France

57 As an instrument of the European Union, the Charter will be of no effect following the UK's departure from the EU. The ECHR, as an instrument of the Council of Europe (of which the UK remains a part) will nonetheless remain.

It was alleged that the applicant had engaged in manipulation in the securities of RCS MediaGroup SpA with a view to making a personal gain. He was prosecuted, convicted and sentenced, but later pardoned. The Italian financial regulator then sought to pursue him for what was, essentially, the same matter through a regulatory action. The court held that a penalty with a potentially punitive purpose (as with regulatory penalties in the UK) is criminal in nature for the purposes of the provisions above.

In practice, this means that there will normally be no 'second bite of the cherry' if the FCA selects a criminal prosecution and the evidence narrowly fails to prove the allegation beyond reasonable doubt. This will be the case even if, for example, a jury acquits by a majority, such as 10 to 2, after a very lengthy retirement or if the prosecution formally offers no evidence after a jury becomes hung on a retrial, as is normally done in such situations.

Conversely, if a regulatory action is pursued and, after a successful conclusion, the FCA feels that the allegation was, in fact, far more serious than they had initially appreciated, and that the evidence is so overwhelming that it would easily satisfy the criminal standard, it will not normally be able to prosecute the same matter as a crime.

Nonetheless, the FCA may take one further step regardless of which route is pursued, namely, to prohibit the individual from engaging in regulated activities at all or in certain respects. This arises out of the fact that only persons considered 'fit and proper' may be authorised to conduct regulated activities; findings of conduct in breach of MAR or the criminal provisions of FSA 2012 may consequently inform the conclusion that the individual is not fit and proper. Thus, for example, in 2014, financial adviser Alok Dhanda was convicted of and imprisoned for fraud. In 2018, the FCA prohibited him from performing any function in relation to any regulated activity. It is open to individuals to challenge prohibition orders by reference to the Upper Tribunal within 28 days of the decision notice being received; Dhanda did not do so.[58]

---

[58] FCA, *Final Notice: Alok Dhanda*, 16 January 2018; https://www.fca.org.uk/publication/final-notices/alok-dhanda-2018.pdf

Relevant Factors

A number of factors appear to influence the FCA's decision-making as to whether to prosecute or bring a regulatory action (whether relating to market manipulation or other forms of market abuse). Factors of particular importance are evidential viability; the gravity of the case (taking account, for instance, of the profit the manipulator made); the suspect's culpability (considering, for example, any breach of trust); and the potential cost of the prosecution.

Since the financial crisis of 2007–2009, the FCA's default position has been to opt for prosecution over regulatory action; a formal decision to this effect was made in 2007. The FCA's general policy is to pursue through the courts 'all those cases where criminal prosecution is appropriate'.[59] Even so, it is still the case that more regulatory actions than criminal prosecutions have been brought for market manipulation in recent years.

The question of whether to pursue a criminal prosecution is largely governed by the Code for Crown Prosecutors.[60] This has two stages: firstly, the evidential stage and, secondly, the public interest stage. The evidential stage must be satisfied before the public interest stage can be considered.

The FCA will have to ask whether, on an objective assessment of the evidence, including the impact of any defence that is likely to be open to the accused, there is sufficient evidence to provide a 'realistic prospect of conviction' against each suspect on each count. This means that a reasonable tribunal of fact, whether jury or magistrates, properly directed and following the law, is more likely than not to find the defendant guilty of the charge(s) brought against them. The FCA will consider the legal admissibility of potential evidence when reaching this decision, including whether it is it caught by any exclusionary rule or discretion.

The FCA will also consider the reliability of the evidence, even if it is theoretically admissible, and whether there are any reasons to doubt its credibility. A case that does not satisfy the evidential stage will proceed no further, no matter how serious it is.

By contrast, regulatory allegations of market manipulation, whether

---

59   FCA *Handbook* at 12.1.2.
60   Ibid.

before the Regulatory Decisions Committee (RDC) or the Upper Tribunal, only have to be established to the civil standard—that is, on the balance of probabilities—rather than beyond reasonable doubt (see *Chapter 7*). Furthermore, when trying to achieve this standard, neither forum applies the strict law of evidence, with its attendant exclusionary rules. Indeed, the Upper Tribunal can admit evidence even if it would not be admissible under the very much less restrictive system of rules found in civil (rather than criminal) trials.[61] This makes achieving a 'positive' result very much easier, as the FCA has sometimes implicitly acknowledged.

For example, in 2017, the FCA apparently considered prosecuting both the chief financial officer and the former financial controller of a company engaged in bet spreading, for criminal market abuse contrary to the FSA 2012. It was alleged that the two men had, *inter alia*, disseminated false and misleading information in documents relating to a publicly listed company. However, the FCA ultimately opted for a regulatory action, in part for evidential reasons: 'The FCA considered carefully whether to pursue criminal charges for market misconduct and decided, in light of the available evidence, that the case should be pursued under the Market Abuse regime'.[62] (The two men were fined and permanently banned from regulated activity).

Assuming that the evidential test is satisfied, the public interest stage has to be considered. In these circumstances, a prosecution will usually be brought *unless* there are public interest factors that outweigh the benefits of such a course of action, such as a potential defendant's extreme youth or physical frailty, the enormous cost entailed in bringing a matter to court (a potentially important consideration in manipulation cases), or the need to protect sources. Significantly, the Crown Prosecution Service (CPS) has noted that, in some cases, the prosecutor may be satisfied that the public interest can be properly served by offering the offender an opportunity to have the matter dealt with by an out-of-court disposal rather than bringing a prosecution. For the FCA, this is particularly important when it comes to dealing with market abuse because, unlike the vast majority of crimes,

---

61   Rule 15(2)(a)(i), Tribunal Procedure (Upper Tribunal) Rules 2008.

62   FCA, 'FCA Bans and Fines Two Individuals for Market Abuse', 7 April 2017; https://www.fca.org.uk/news/press-releases/fca-bans-and-fines-two-individuals-market-abuse

there is a very real, but still formal, alternative to criminal prosecution, in the form of a regulatory action.

Perhaps because of this, paragraphs 12.3.1 to 12.3.4 of the FCA's *Handbook* expressly identify considerations that might be relevant when making a decision to prosecute, some of which are independent of those identified by the Director of Public Prosecutions (head of the CPS), although many overlap. Among them are: the seriousness of the misconduct and the prospect of a significant sentence if prosecuted as a crime; the effect of the misconduct on the market, particularly where there is significant disruption or damage to market confidence; the extent of any gain made or loss avoided; whether the person is being or has been voluntarily cooperative with the FCA in taking corrective measures; whether an individual's misconduct involves dishonesty or an abuse of a position of authority or trust; and whether, where the misconduct was carried out by a group, the individual played a leading role in what occurred.

In more general terms, the degree of 'culpability' manifested by the alleged manipulator is a particularly important factor when deciding whether to have recourse to a regulatory action or prosecution. For example, in November 2017, the FCA fined a bond dealer £60,090 for market abuse in contravention of section 118(5) FSMA. In the summer of 2014 the dealer had carried out a strategy of entering quotes on the BrokerTec inter-dealer trading platform that influenced other market participants' quoting behaviour. He then benefited from the price movements that followed. The FCA expressly accepted that his market abuse had not been committed deliberately: 'Although the Authority has concluded that Mr [C] did not intend to commit market abuse, he should have realised that his behaviour constituted market abuse'.[63]

As noted, another important policy factor when making the choice as to forum is the potential cost of a criminal prosecution, both to the regulator itself and to the public purse (via the cost of a trial). Even prosecuting a single defendant can result in a lengthy hearing. For example, in the summer of 2015, Tom Hayes' trial for LIBOR manipulation lasted 47 days

---

63   FCA, *Final Notice*, 22 November 2017.

at Southwark Crown Court. Other cases, with multiple defendants, have lasted even longer.

Suspect Co-operation

If the FCA decides that the criminal course would be the appropriate option, a person may nonetheless avoid prosecution or benefit from a reduction in sentence by co-operating with the regulator's investigation. Agreements to this end are provided for in Part 2, Chapter 2 of the Serious Organised Crime and Police Act 2005 (SOCPA). Under these provisions, the suspect might, for example, receive a significantly reduced sentence if he or she admits the offence, pleads guilty, and gives evidence against others. Such agreements should not be entered into lightly. The experiences of the alleged LIBOR manipulator Tom Hayes are indicative of both the potential benefits and risks.

In early December 2012, the USA authorities indicted Hayes and, on 11 December, he was arrested in the UK. He then engaged with domestic prosecuting authorities and, on 23 March 2013, entered into a SOCPA agreement, offering assistance in the form of full and frank admissions. These were made in a series of interviews over the following two months and to the effect that Hayes had knowingly acted dishonestly. He was charged by the UK authorities on 18 June 2013. However, in October, Hayes withdrew from the SOCPA process and pleaded 'not guilty' at trial.

Inevitably, the SOCPA interviews formed a substantial part of the prosecution case against Hayes. For example, he had stated: 'Well look, I mean, it's a dishonest scheme, isn't it? … And I was part of the dishonest scheme, so obviously I was being dishonest.'[64] However, Mr Hayes contended that these admissions to dishonesty had been prompted by a fear of extradition to the USA and its harsh sentences and prisons. In order to be charged in the UK, and so avoid that outcome, he had needed to admit wrongdoing. At trial, and despite the statements in the earlier interviews, Hayes' case was that he had not been acting dishonestly by the ordinary standards of

---

64   See Liam Vaughan and Gavin Finch, 'Libor Scandal: The Bankers Who Fixed the World's Most Important Number', *The Guardian*, 18 January 2017; https://www.theguardian.com/business/2017/jan/18/libor-scandal-the-bankers-who-fixed-the-worlds-most-important-number

reasonable and honest people (see *Chapter 4*). Even so, he was convicted, and the trial judge expressly noted that the defendant's decision to abandon the SOCPA process meant that he was not able to avail himself of a mitigating factor that would have resulted in a very much shorter sentence than that eventually imposed. Indeed, it has been suggested that his reneging on the agreement helps to explain the exceptionally heavy sentence imposed on him (albeit slightly reduced on appeal).

CHAPTER 4

Market Manipulation as a Criminal Offence

Introduction

Legislation specifically proscribing market manipulation has existed in some parts of the world since the 1930s. The USA was one of the first to introduce such provisions after the Wall Street Crash of 1929, in the form of section 17(a) of the Securities Act of 1933, and sections 9(a)(2) and 10(b) of the Securities Exchange Act of 1934. The United Kingdom was comparatively late amongst common law jurisdictions with developed securities markets to enact a full regime of specialist legislation. The first statutory offence of market manipulation was created by the Financial Services Act 1986 (FSA 1986), although it had some limited statutory antecedents from the 1930s and 1950s.

Nevertheless, market abuse was not a totally unregulated area, even in the 1800s. Both common law and professional disciplinary action had been employed to preserve markets from such misconduct for almost two centuries before the FSA 1986, if not always very effectively. For instance, prosecutions were occasionally brought for ordinary criminal offences committed against a backdrop of market manipulation. An early example occurred as a result of the 'Great Stock Exchange Fraud' of 1814. The fraudster, Charles Random de Berenger, posed as an aide-de-camp to an English general in Dover, where he falsely began to spread the news that Napoleon had been killed and the war with France was over. Two fully-uniformed, but equally bogus, Bourbon officers supported his account by presenting handbills in London. The morning the news was received, various government securities on the LSE soared. However, by afternoon, the government had confirmed that the news was a fabrication and the price of the affected stocks immediately sank back to their previous levels.

The Committee of the Stock Exchange launched an investigation and quickly discovered that more than £1.1 million in two government-based stocks, most purchased the previous week, had been sold at the peak of the spike in prices. (De Berenger's scheme was effectively a 'bull raid'.) Subsequently, de Berenger and others connected with the hoax were arrested, charged with fraud, convicted, and punished with a year's imprisonment and a heavy fine. On appeal, Lord Ellenborough confirmed (Le Blanc, Bayley and Dampier LJJ agreeing) that, as a matter of law, giving a saleable commodity in the market a 'fictitious price, by means of false rumours' constituted a fraud levelled against the public.[1]

Eighty years later, in *Scott v Brown, Doering, McNab & Co* [1892] 2 QB 724, the court considered an agreement to purchase shares in a company. The alleged objective was to induce would-be buyers to believe there was a market for such shares, and that they were of greater value than was really the case. Lopes LJ, *obiter*, considered that such an agreement was not only illegal but 'might be made the subject of an indictment for conspiracy'. His Lordship noted that although *De Berenger* had involved an indictment for conspiracy conducted by false rumours, he could see 'no substantial distinction between false rumours and false and fictitious acts; the price of the shares in this case was artificial'.

The common law therefore appears to have been capable of addressing both information- and transaction-based manipulation. Indeed, it was on the basis of the common law offence of conspiracy to defraud that, as recently as 2015, Tom Hayes was tried for LIBOR manipulation. At the time of his offending, between 2006 and 2010, manipulation of benchmarks was not a specialist criminal offence.[2]

Furthermore, some non-specialist statutory offences might also be relevant to market manipulation, even if they have yet to be invoked for such purposes. This is of significance where the specialist provisions had not entered into force at the time of the alleged misconduct. Most important in this respect is the Fraud Act 2006 (FA), which came into effect on 15 January 2007. Section 1 FA defines fraud as breach of one of the FA's three following

---

1   *De Berenger* (1814) 3 M&S 67, 105 ER 536.
2   But now see section 91 FSA 2012.

provisions, each of which sets out a different means of committing fraud. These are, respectively, making a false representation (section 2); failing to disclose information (section 3); and abuse of position (section 4). Common to each is that the relevant person acts dishonestly and, in engaging in the particular conduct, intends either to make a gain for themselves or another person, or to cause loss to another or expose another person to loss.

In theory, there is nothing to prevent someone who had, for example, disseminated false information over the internet or via a Regulatory Information Service announcement as part of a 'pump and dump' scheme from being prosecuted under the Fraud Act, just as they could be under section 89 FSA 2012.[3]

Specialist Legislation in the UK

Market manipulation was first made a statutory offence by section 47 of the FSA 1986. In effect, there were three means of committing the offence: first, by knowingly or recklessly making a 'statement, promise or forecast' which is 'misleading, false or deceptive'; secondly, by dishonestly concealing material facts; and thirdly, by doing an act or engaging in a course of conduct 'which creates a false or misleading impression as to the market in or the price or value of any investments'. It was a further element of each that the purpose of the relevant words or conduct was to induce another person to deal with an investment in a particular way.

The foundations for the current criminal offences can already be seen in the provision for both information- and transaction-based manipulation. Section 47 FSA 1986 had its own earlier roots, namely in the Prevention of Fraud (Investments) Acts of 1939 and 1958. Those provisions did not, however, extend to transaction-based manipulation, focusing instead on statements (and the like), and 'dishonest concealment of material facts'. The intended causing of loss was also beyond their remit.

These provisions were repealed by the more expansive FSA 1986, which in turn was replaced by the FSMA. In substance, section 397 FSMA reproduced section 47 FSA 1986 but with less ambiguous drafting. A key distinction

---

3   Anderson et al, *A Practitioner's Guide*, at 167.

from the earlier provision was that section 397(1)(b) made clear that any dishonest concealment of material facts need not occur in connection with a 'statement, promise or forecast', as long as the purpose in making it was a relevant inducement. Section 397 FSMA also provides for more sophisticated defences relating to transaction-based offences or (in effect) knowingly false statements.

Specifically, if a defendant could show that they were seeking to act in conformity with certain standards or rules around, for example, price stabilisation, the relevant offence could not be made out. As with section 47 FSA 1986, under section 397 FSMA, the relevant conduct also had to either occur or have its effect within the United Kingdom.

In its turn, section 397 was repealed by the FSA 2012, which came into force on 1 April 2013. The FSA 2012 sets out the present specialist criminal regime governing market manipulation, with the current offences laid down in sections 89–91. These are: making false or misleading statements (section 89); creating false or misleading impressions (section 90); and, for the first time (and in response to the LIBOR scandal), making false or misleading statements or creating a false or misleading impression in relation to specified financial benchmarks (section 91). These will be discussed in further detail below.

It also bears noting that, in July 2016, as the MAR came into effect, the EU's Directive on Criminal Sanctions for Market Abuse (CSMAD) became operative as well. The CSMAD aimed to update the EU Member States' criminal regimes in the light of technological change and the financial crisis of 2007–2009. As CSMAD took the form of a directive, Member States were required to pass national implementing measures to bring it into effect. However, the UK (along with Denmark) did not opt into the CSMAD and, instead, undertook to make any necessary changes to their existing criminal market abuse regimes on a national basis. In the UK, these were necessarily fairly modest, as in many respects the UK's criminal regime, as set out under Part 7 FSA 2012, was already more robust than that anticipated in CSMAD.[4]

---

4   See Mark Hoban (Financial Secretary to the Treasury), Ministerial Statement to the House of Commons: 'Criminal Sanctions Directive on Market Abuse', 20 February 2012; https://publications.parliament.uk/pa/cm201212/cmhansrd/cm120220/wmstext/120220m0001.htm

Because of the relatively recent nature of their enactment, there are only three cases in which any of the market manipulation offence provisions of the FSA 2012 have been mentioned. None deals with their proper interpretation.[5] Nevertheless, similarities in wording and context mean that some of the decisions made with regard to section 47 FSA 1986 and section 397 FSMA will continue to be significant under FSA 2012.[6]

Some Preliminary Points

A number of preliminary points can be made with regard to the complex criminal provisions set out in Part 7 FSA 2012, if only to facilitate comprehension.

Corporate Liability

An offence contrary to sections 89, 90 or 91 may be committed by a 'person'.[7] There is nothing in the FSA 2012 to displace the ordinary legislative meaning of that term in accordance with the Interpretation Act 1978, namely to 'include [...] a body of persons corporate or unincorporate'.[8] As such, each of the market manipulation offences under FSA 2012 may be committed by a company[9] and not only by natural persons, such as its employees.

Dishonesty

Dishonesty is an essential element to many acquisitive criminal offences.[10] However, the only market manipulation offence to which it applies is section 89(1)(c) FSA 2012, namely the dishonest concealment of material facts.

---

5   *FCA v Skinner* [2019] EWHC 392 (Ch) (application to withdraw admissions; section 89); *Molton Street Capital LLP v Shooters Hill Capital Partners LLP* [2015] EWHC 3419 (Comm) (contract—implied term; section 89); *Government of the United States of America v Sarao* (extradition; section 90).

6   See Rider et al, *Market Abuse and Insider Dealing*, at 113.

7   This may be contrasted with section 52 of the Criminal Justice Act 1993, which provides that the offence of insider dealing that it established may be committed only by 'an individual'—that is, a *natural* person.

8   See section 5 and Schedule 1.

9   See Rider et al, *Market Abuse and Insider Dealing*, at 113.

10 See e.g. section 1, Theft Act 1968; sections 2–4, Fraud Act 2006; and conspiracy to defraud at common law; cf section 52 Criminal Justice Act 1993.

Despite its narrow application for present purposes, dishonesty needs careful consideration due to its definitional complexity. Until 2017, dishonesty was defined by the Court of Appeal decision in *Ghosh* [1982] 3 WLR 110, which established a two-fold objective/subjective test. The first step was to decide whether what was done was dishonest according to the ordinary standards of reasonable and honest people. If so, it had to be asked whether the defendant himself must have realised that what he was doing was dishonest by those standards.

However, in *Ivey v Genting Casinos (UK) Ltd* [2017] 3 WLR 1212, a civil case brought in the context of alleged cheating at a casino, the Supreme Court took the opportunity to reconsider this definition. The court expressed concern about some of *Ghosh*'s ramifications: for example, it effectively meant that the more warped a person's own standards of honesty, the less likely their conviction would be, because they would be unlikely to recognise their own dishonesty. It was also thought highly undesirable that the meaning of dishonesty should vary between civil and criminal forums, as was then the case.

Strictly speaking, the Supreme Court's comments on dishonesty in criminal matters in *Ivey* were *obiter dicta*, as it was a civil case. However, in *Pabon* [2018] EWCA Crim 420, the Court of Appeal accepted its direct application to the criminal context by stating, 'in the light of *Ivey* … that second leg of the *Ghosh* test has been disapproved as not correctly representing the law'. The Court of Appeal went on: 'It is therefore apparent that the jury were directed, on the key issue of dishonesty, on a basis more favourable to the appellant than if he was tried today'.[11]

Following *Ivey*, where dishonesty is in issue, a court must first ascertain the state of the defendant's subjective knowledge or belief (whether reasonably held or not) as to the facts of a case. Once this has been established, whether the defendant's conduct was dishonest is to be determined simply by applying the objective standards of ordinary, honest people to those facts.

The objective test is, however, not without its own difficulties. For instance, one of the grounds of appeal advanced in the LIBOR manipulation

---

11   *Pabon* at para 63.

case of *Hayes* [2015] EWCA Crim 1944; [2018] 1 Cr App R 10 was that the defence had been wrongly precluded from putting forward matters relevant to the objective limb of *Ghosh*, as then applied. The appellant argued that he should have been allowed to adduce evidence on, for example, the ethos of the banking system at the time of his impugned conduct; the prevalence of commercial LIBOR requests from traders to LIBOR submitters; and the attitude of the Bank of England and the FSAu (now the FCA) towards LIBOR—in particular, their refusal to actively regulate it despite knowing that it suffered from flawed governance and was not very accurate. Essentially, the appellant was arguing that the objective standard should not be set by reference to the ordinary 'man in the street', but rather by a 'person in the market'.

The Court of Appeal firmly rejected this approach. Some of the proposed evidence would have been relevant to the second, subjective limb (now no longer applicable, following *Ivey*), but it had no bearing on the objective test. Indeed, the court considered that accepting the principle proposed, of fixing the objective test by reference to market participants, might gravely affect the proper conduct of business, as markets sometimes unwittingly abandon ordinary and proper standards of honesty.[12]

Tom Hayes was of course prosecuted for conspiracy to defraud—a broad common law offence of which dishonesty is a central element. However, as noted above, the only offence under Part 7 of the FSA 2012 for which dishonesty is required is dishonest concealment of material facts contrary to section 89(1)(c). Even without the second limb of dishonesty, this does not make it an easy offence to prove, as will be discussed further below.

Recklessness

For several of the offences listed under Part 7 FSA 2012, recklessness, rather than intention, will suffice as the mental element. This has been judicially defined to mean that a defendant must be shown to have subjectively appreciated the risk presented by their behaviour, but carried on regardless, before

---

12   *Hayes* at paras 32–33.

they can be found criminally responsible.[13] It is not enough that someone else might have seen that there was such a risk if the defendant did not.[14]

It has been suggested that little in fact turns on the difference, given that a jury will often assess what the defendant foresaw on the basis of what they themselves would have foreseen in the circumstances. However, the present authors consider that there is a relevant difference. Under the current subjective test, the jury will have to consider the credibility of the defendant's denial of having in fact foreseen the risk, upon which other evidence (for example, as to good character) may also bear.

As a result, the key question under the Part 7 offences involving recklessness is whether the defendant foresaw the possibility that a statement they made or impression they created might be false or misleading, and then proceeded to make the statement or engage in the conduct creating the impression regardless.

This then invites the question as to how likely that possibility has to be for the associated conduct to be reckless. In effect, this involves balancing the probability of the risk against any justification for taking it: it may be reasonable, and therefore not reckless, to accept a higher probability of risk if the grounds for doing so are strong. An example would be a surgeon undertaking a difficult operation, with its own possibility of complications, without which the patient would very likely die.

This approach is reflected in an early case under section 13(1) of the Prevention of Fraud (Investment) Act 1958. *Grunwald* [1963] 1 QB 935 concerned the making of reckless statements in order to purchase or sell shares. Paull J considered the necessary degree of possibility in some detail and concluded that it would cover 'rash' statements where the maker was heedless of the fact that he or she had no real basis of facts to support them.

Recklessness was also in issue in the FSAu's first contested market manipulation prosecution, *Rigby and Bailey*, in 2005. The defendants were former

---

13   See *G* [2003] UKHL 50; [2004] 1 AC 1034, where the House of Lords effectively abandoned 'objective recklessness', which had been applied to some offences since *Metropolitan Police Commissioner v Caldwell* [1982] AC 341. The House instead favoured the subjective approach of *Cunningham* [1957] 2 QB 396.

14   This was the alternative standard that applied under *Caldwell*, above.

executives of the call-centre software firm AIT. Each faced trial at South-wark Crown Court on alternative counts of either knowingly or recklessly making misleading statements to investors contrary to section 397(1)(a) or (c) FSMA.[15]

The case centred on an interim statement issued via an RNS to the LSE on 2 May 2002 in which AIT announced that it had had a 'satisfactory end' to the financial year. It forecast a profit in line with market expecta-tions of £6.7m. The FSAu's case was that this statement was issued after the defendants had persuaded the company's auditors that it had won three contracts worth £4.8m, at the last minute. In reality, although this was not entirely fanciful, these were not legally binding agreements as side-letters not shown to the accountants made clear. The provisional agreements fell through within a few weeks of the announcement.

As a result, on 31 May 2002, a profit warning was issued announcing that the 2 May statement was no longer accurate, leading to a £1.1m shortfall in profit. The warning also noted that short-term cash requirements were unlikely to be covered by AIT's available borrowing facilities and other cash resources. The company's share price immediately fell from 492.5p to 96.5p. Another negative trading update followed soon after, on 13 June, partly because the company had failed to satisfy itself that the value of a licence 'agreement' worth £2.5m could properly be recognised in the year-end results. The company said that there would be a further shortfall in revenue and profit. The share price fell again from 105p to 38.5p.[16] As a consequence, 94% of the firm's market value had been wiped off since early May.[17]

Bailey was acquitted of the more serious charge of knowingly making misleading statements, while the jury could not agree with respect to Rigby and so that count was left to lie. However, both men were convicted of the alternative charge of doing so recklessly. (Had the 'contracts' been a com-plete fabrication, as opposed to negotiated but non-binding agreements,

15 See generally *Rigby and Bailey* [2005] EWCA Crim 3487; [2006] 2 Cr App R 36.
16 Paul Barnes, 'Insider Dealing and Market Abuse: The UK's Record on Enforcement' (2011) 39 *International Journal of Law, Crime and Justice* 174–189 at 184.
17 Simon Bowers, 'AIT Boss Rigby Becomes First To Be Jailed for Market Abuse', *The Guardian*, 7 October 2002; https://www.theguardian.com/business/2005/oct/08/4

that outcome would likely have been different.) Each was sentenced to imprisonment, at first instance to respective terms of two years (Bailey) and three and ½ years (Rigby). Their sentences were subsequently reduced to nine months and 18 months respectively, with the Court of Appeal stressing that they had been convicted of reckless rather than knowing conduct.

Another example of recklessness arose in the 2011 case of Stuart Pearson.[18] Pearson was a qualified and experienced accountant, and former chief executive of AIM-listed investment services company Langbar International (Langbar). That case centred around claims Pearson had made through official LSE RNS announcements in 2005, as well as to a hedge fund manager personally. Those claims were to the effect that Langbar had substantial assets held by Banco do Brasil, some of which were being transferred to Langbar directly. These claims pushed up Langbar's share price and encouraged further investment. However, trading was suspended in October 2005, when Langbar's value was questioned. In November 2005, Langbar announced that it could not establish the existence of, nor its entitlement to, the previously claimed Banco do Brasil deposits, and the company subsequently collapsed. As the SFO, which investigated and prosecuted the matter, later noted: '[Langbar] had no money and its shares no real value.' Institutional and private investors lost tens of millions of pounds.

At the time of Langbar's collapse, Pearson had only been with the company for six months. Yet by that time, Langbar had already been the subject of a much longer-standing, and highly sophisticated, fraud scheme engineered from abroad. Pearson was a very minor, late arriving, and peripheral figure in what occurred. Nevertheless, his professional background meant that he would have been fully aware of the strict requirements demanded of companies publishing information to the market. The jury was also shown evidence suggesting that he had disregarded a phone call from a concerned banker at the London branch of Banco do Brasil, who told him that there were no records of Langbar's declared funds being on deposit. This and other warnings should have prevented him issuing what transpired to be misleading statements to investors, albeit that he did not do so deliberately.

---

18   See generally Julia Kollewe, 'Former Langbar Chief Jailed over Fraud', *The Guardian*, 20 June 2011; https://www.theguardian.com/law/2011/jun/20/former-langbar-chief-jailed-fraud

He appreciated the risk that the deposits might not exist, but did not know they were absent.

Territoriality

As with most offences, territorial jurisdiction must be satisfied before the offence-creating provisions of Part 7 FSA 2012 apply. In this regard, sections 89 and 90 largely replicate section 397 FSMA, restricting application of those offences to cases where, in summary, the wrongful conduct occurred or would have effect in the UK.[19] As such, although there must be a nexus with the UK, conduct or statements occurring outside it can be captured.[20]

The territorial scope of the benchmark-related offences in section 91 is slightly narrower. Section 91(1) addresses the making of misleading statements intended to be used in setting a 'relevant benchmark'. Section 91(1), however, applies only where the statement is made 'in or from the United Kingdom or to a person in the United Kingdom'.[21] Section 91(2) deals with conduct creating a false or misleading impression in the knowledge it may be used in setting a 'relevant benchmark'. The broader scope of sections 89 and 90 operates here, such that the conduct will be caught if the relevant conduct occurs in the UK, or the false or misleading impression is created there.

'Relevant' Agreements, Investments and Benchmarks

Sections 89–91 deal with statements or conduct affecting only a 'relevant agreement', 'relevant investment', or 'relevant benchmark'. Section 93(3)-(5) defines each of these terms, in effect providing that an agreement, investment or benchmark is 'relevant' if the Treasury has made an order so specifying or, with respect to agreements, the agreement entails a specified activity. The definition of a 'relevant agreement' is also tied to that of a 'relevant investment', as the agreement must relate to such an investment. The purpose of such an approach is to permit flexibility within the criminal regime, so

---

19   See sections 89(4) and 90(10).

20   Extradition proceedings may then be used to enable prosecution within the UK if the accused remains outside it although how this might operate in relation to EU countries after the UK's departure was unclear at the time of printing.

21   See 91(5).

that it may develop as the financial markets do (although, in order to be fair, such legislative adaption should of course not operate retrospectively).

The current 'relevant' matters are set out in the Financial Services Act 2012 (Misleading Statements and Impressions) Order 2013 (FSAMSIO). As regards agreements, the list includes, *inter alia*, managing, or acting as a trustee or depositary of, an alternative investment fund; establishing a collective investment or pension scheme; and dealing in investments as a principal or agent in relation to a contract of insurance.[22] There are presently eight specified benchmarks, namely LIBOR, the ICE Swap Rate, the Sterling Overnight Index Average (SONIA), the Repurchase Overnight Index Average (RONIA'), WM/Reuters London 4 pm Closing Spot Rate, London Gold Fixing, LBMA Silver Price, and the ICE Brent Index.[23]

The only specified investments are the 'controlled investments' set out in Part 2 of the Financial Services and Markets Act 2000 (Financial Promotion) Order 2005/1529.[24] These include government and public securities, options, futures, CFDs and emissions allowances, among many others.

It should be noted that, while there is overlap between the scope of the criminal regime and that of the MAR, the financial instruments are not necessarily the same, due to the different means by which they are defined by the respective legislative schemes.

A Precautionary Approach

Each of the offences in Part 7 FSA is focussed not on the outcome of the wrongdoer's conduct, but the fact of that conduct in light of what could be the outcome. So, albeit that an individual may, for example, be induced to enter into an investment by a misleading statement, it is not necessary that that be proven to have occurred for the offence to be successfully prosecuted. Similarly, there is no requirement that the wrongdoer or anyone else actually make a profit or loss as a result of what they have done. Section 90 comes closest to this, by providing in subsection (3)-(4) that an offence will be committed if a wrongdoer intends, by creating a false or misleading

---

22 See article 2 FSAMSIO.

23 See article 3 FSAMSIO.

24 See articles 1 and 4 FSAMSIO.

impression, to make a gain for himself or herself or another, or to cause another loss or exposure to loss.[25]

Nonetheless, the outcome of the wrongdoer's conduct is likely to have some bearing on any decision to prosecute, based on the Code for Crown Prosecutors (applicable to the FCA). The ability to prove that an individual has relied on the wrongdoer's conduct to their detriment or the wrongdoer's gain may both bolster the prosecution case evidentially, as well as increasing the public interest in prosecution due to the harm caused.

The FSA 2012 Offences

Section 89

Section 89 deals with the making of misleading statements and the dishonest concealment of material facts—what is often termed 'information-based manipulation'. It effectively replaces section 397(2) FSMA.

Section 89(1) FSA 2012 means that the offence-creating provision in section 89(2) applies in three distinct circumstances: where a person makes a statement, either (1) 'knowing' that it is a materially false or misleading, or (2) acting 'recklessly' as to whether this is the case, or where that person (3) dishonestly conceals material facts (whether in connection with a false or misleading statement or not). There are several key aspects to each of these applicability provisions, meriting more detailed examination and analysis.

First, in the first two situations, there must be a statement that is 'false' or 'misleading'. Whether a statement is false or misleading is a question of fact. By analogy with the interpretation of section 397 FSMA, the statement must be false or misleading at the time it was made.[26] The helpful explanation given in *Archbold* is that a statement 'is false or misleading if it is objectively incorrect, or if it is objectively correct but omits material information so that it is misleading as a whole'.[27]

Secondly, the statement must be false or misleading 'in a material respect'.

---

25 See section 90(3)-(4). The offence is also committed where the wrongdoer is aware that creating the false or misleading impression is likely to cause such a gain, loss or exposure.

26 See *Blackstone's Criminal Practice* (2019, Oxford University Press) at B7.47.

27 See *Archbold Criminal Pleading and Practice* (2019, Sweet & Maxwell) at 30–75.

This will be the case 'if that respect is or would be expected to have an effect on the person intended to be induced to enter into a relevant agreement or investment'.[28] As a result, false information about trivial and peripheral matters may be outside the ambit of section 89. For example, consider a case in which an obsessive athlete attempts to 'ramp' a company's shares, in which he already had a substantial holding, by falsely announcing on the internet that its CEO had run 100 metres in under 11 seconds. This would arguably not fall within section 89, as although the statement is false, it would not be expected that the speed at which the CEO runs would have an effect on an investor's choice whether or not to invest in the company.

Materiality would operate in the same manner with respect to concealment. Some general, if oblique, guidance may be obtained from the law of contract. In *Dimmock v Hallett* (1866) LR 2 Ch App 21, an estate including three parcels of land was auctioned off. The advertisement and particulars for the auction stated that each parcel was let out to paying tenants. However, it was never mentioned that the tenants had already given notice to quit. The eventual buyer sought rescission of the contract for, *inter alia*, misrepresentation. The Chancery Appeal Court held that in these circumstances, telling a half truth about the existing tenants constituted good grounds for rescission. Turner LJ observed that the purchaser would be led to suppose that he was purchasing farms 'with continuing tenancies at fixed rents, whereas he would, in fact, have to find tenants immediately after the completion of his purchase'. The fact that notice had been given by the tenants put a completely different complexion on the vendor's (technically accurate) statement.

To consider a market manipulation context, suppose a defence firm, XYZ PLC, is in the market to supply a new frigate to the navy. A decision by the Ministry of Defence is expected any day. Someone holding shares in XYZ reminds an internet investment forum that a decision on the issue is imminent, and then announces (truthfully) that XYZ have started urgently refurbishing the frigate slipway in the yard where they would make the warship, if their bid were successful, without also stating that the company

---

28   Ibid.

had been ordered to do this by the Health and Safety Executive because of serious safety concerns. In the absence of this information, readers of the statement might interpret it as an indication that the company was confident that the order was 'in the bag' and invest in its shares accordingly.

The Mental State behind the Statement or Concealment

For each variant of the section 89 offence, there are effectively two mental states to be proven: first, that involved in making the statement or concealing the material facts, and secondly, that pertaining to the effect of doing so. For example, section 89(2) may be contravened where an individual: (1) knows their statement is false or misleading; and (2) either (a) intends that another may be relevantly induced, or (b) is reckless as to such inducement. Similarly, an individual may dishonestly conceal material facts, and then either intend or be reckless as to another's inducement in connection with an investment.

For a hypothetical example, suppose that an investor has been conducting careful research into ABC PLC, a relatively small company that has had a slew of bad news, and whose equities are now trading as penny shares on the LSE. The investor concludes that the bad news has been greatly exaggerated, and that the company has substantial assets and bright prospects. At 2 pm he decides to take a CFD with a maximum liability of £50,000 on its share price increasing from 10p to 13p a share. In the last hour of trading on the LSE, he decides to increase his exposure further, but this time by directly purchasing a tranche of the company's shares. He invests £40,000. The effect of this purchase is to drive up the thinly traded low-value shares to 12p a share by the close of the market. This arguably constitutes an act creating an impression as to the value of the shares—but not one he intended to make. Nor is it clear that the impression was false or misleading, insofar as the investor took an informed view as to the possible upturn of the company's futures. However, if the following morning, the investor realises that he or she can close his CFD position and then makes a tidy profit from doing so, the FCA may well look at these transactions through the lens of section 90(3), even if it eventually concludes there are no prospects of conviction. (The regulatory situation might well be different).

By contrast, suppose that the same investor makes and cancels dozens of orders in the same equity, in the final hour of business, with the same result on its share price. He does so with a specific view to raising that price, while always intending to close his position. The timing and speed of the transactions may provide evidence of that intention, such that a section 90 offence could be made out.

Inducement

Section 89(2) requires that there be an 'intention of inducing', or recklessness as to whether the statement or concealment 'may induce, another person ...

(a)   to enter into or offer to enter into, or to refrain from entering or offering to enter into, a relevant agreement, or

(b)   to exercise, or refrain from exercising, any rights conferred by a relevant investment.'

(As to the meaning of 'relevant agreement' and 'relevant investment' see the discussion above.)

It is not necessary that a person to whom a statement is made be the same person who is intended to be, or may by recklessness be, induced to some action. For example, Trader X may give information to Trader Y, who Trader X knows will not be interested in a particular type of investment but who works closely with Trader Z, who will be. Trader Y (having satisfied herself that it seemed accurate) may pass this information on to Trader Z, who then does enter into an investment, as Trader X intended. Alternatively, the communication may occur across a broadcast medium, such as an RNS, a web-based chat forum, or even Twitter.

An Illustrative Case

To consider a simple illustration: A purchases a tranche of 'penny shares' in PQR PLC on the LSE MM. She then goes onto six web investor chatrooms under an assumed name and announces that she has firm information that the company is about to be the subject of a takeover bid by a cash-rich private limited company which is keen to secure an LSE listing. This is clearly a 'statement'. A knows that this is nonsense, so it is 'false' and, given its subject matter, it is false in a 'material respect'. As a result, section 89(1)(a) is satisfied and section 89(2) applies. A placed the notices to induce others to enter into a 'relevant agreement' (a share purchase) under the definition set out in section 93(3), satisfying section 89(2)(a) and making out the offence.

Stock Promotion

Arguably, there is a potentially grey, and certainly difficult, area between legitimate stock 'promotion' and illegitimate market 'manipulation' contrary to section 89 FSA 2012. When it comes to small companies, it is among a CEO's many duties to promote the company and so enable it to raise money if it issues new shares. It is also natural for active investors to be optimistic, if not positively bullish, about the stocks that they acquire or keep. Furthermore, there is no law against announcing this on public forums, including on the Internet. Suppose that this prompts a movement in share price that is favourable to the maker of such a statement and of which he or she then takes advantage. Whether this is a facet of legitimate promotion or illicit manipulation will depend on the mental states motivating the person's conduct. That is a matter of which there will rarely be direct evidence and, more commonly, must be established by piecing together the circumstances in which the conduct occurred.

For example, an investor who purchases shares in XYZ PLC and then publicises via an Internet chat-room a truthful and positive piece of information that, for some reason, had previously been largely ignored by the market, does not commit a criminal offence, even if it leads to the shares rising and the investor eventually making a profit. The statement was not false. Similarly, if the same investor publicises an untrue piece of positive information, in the same manner, and with the same result, but genuinely believing it to be entirely true, no offence is committed; there is no knowledge of falsity. Finally, if the investor knowingly disseminates untrue information, without intending, or having foreseen that there was a risk that it would induce other people to do certain things, no offence would be committed — although this combination or mental states is likely to be rare.

In practice, the FCA is likely to view certain behaviour patterns as indicative, for instance, that a dealer did not genuinely believe in the case for investing in the securities concerned, and so may be manipulating the market. For example, an investor who sells much of their own holding in a particular stock, especially one of the 'penny share' type, while simultaneously encouraging others to buy it, via an internet forum with a major following, and in which they are a respected commentator, is likely to be viewed as suspicious. As a matter of prudence, any investor who holds shares that they actively promote through the media would also be well advised to declare their interest when doing so, especially if they then liquidate those shares at a profit. Indeed, a failure to do so might, on its own, be deemed a regulatory offence by dint of article 12(2)(d) MAR (see *Chapter 6*), even if entirely true.

Section 90: Misleading Impressions

Section 90(1) FSA 2012, which replaced section 397(3) FSMA, criminalises 'any act or … course of conduct which creates a false or misleading impression as to the market in or the price or value of any relevant investments' in circumstances described in the following subsections. In contrast with section 89, it proscribes 'transaction-based' manipulation. It is roughly the criminal equivalent of the regulatory provision in article 12(1)(a)(i) MAR, which proscribes entering into a transaction or placing an order to trade which gives, or is likely to give, false or misleading signals as to the supply of, demand for, or price of, a financial instrument (see *Chapter 6*).

In essence, the following prerequisites must be established for the section 90 offence to be made out:

(1)   there must be an act or course of conduct by the defendant;
(2)   that act or course of conduct must:
    (a)   be intended to create an impression, which is false or misleading; and
    (b)   actually create that impression;
(3)   that impression must go to the market in, or price or value of, a 'relevant investment'; and
(4)   the defendant must either:

(a) intend, by creating the impression, to induce another to deal with that investment or rights associated with it in certain ways, or

(b) know that, or be reckless as to whether, the impression is false or misleading, and either intend or be aware that, by creating it, a likely result is that the defendant or another will gain, or that another will be caused or exposed to loss.[29]

The terms 'gain' and 'loss' are defined by further provisions of section 90. Both terms extend only to monetary or proprietary effects, whether temporary or permanent. A gain includes 'a gain by keeping what one has, as well as a gain by getting what one does not have', while a loss correspondingly includes 'a loss by not getting what one might get, as well as a loss by parting with what one has'.[30]

The phrase 'any act or ... course of conduct' is obviously very broad and appears apt to extend to most forms of transaction, whether a single instance or a series of deals. Significantly, this should include those occasioned by HFT,[31] regarding which concerns were raised earlier in this book. For example, purchasing a large tranche of securities just before the close of the market would be an 'act'. Similarly, placing and then quickly cancelling numerous orders would constitute a 'course of conduct'.

The act or course of conduct must then create a false or misleading impression. Under section 397 FSMA, such an impression would have to have been one drawn by a 'regular user of the market'. This is not mentioned in section 90 FSA 2012, which was according to its Explanatory Note, designed to 'replicate [...] and extend [...] the effect of section 397(3) of FSMA'. The reason for this textual change is not apparent, however it seems to recognise that unsophisticated investors deserve, too, to be protected from manipulative conduct.

---

29 See section 90(1)-(4).

30 See section 90(6)-(8).

31 Fisher et al, 'Criminal Forms of High Frequency Trading', at 113.

Mental Elements

As with the section 89 offence, there is some complexity around the mental elements to be proven. The drafting of section 90(1) alone suggests that a person must intend to create a false or misleading impression, insofar as (a) refers to an intention 'to create *the* impression' (referring back to the 'false or misleading impression' in (1)).

However, when examined as a whole, the present authors suggest correct reading of section 90(1) is that the person must intend to create *an* impression, which is in fact false or misleading. This is so because the offence is not completed unless the case falls within either or both of subsections 90(2) and (3). Subsection 3(a) contemplates that the person may simply be reckless as to whether the impression made is false or misleading. It is difficult to reconcile an intention to make a false or misleading impression with recklessness as to its false or misleading nature.

Moreover, the first reading would not require that the impression in fact be false or misleading, such that it is difficult to see how any harm could be caused. For these reasons, it is suggested that the better view is that the person must intend to create a specific impression, either knowing that, or being reckless as to whether, it is false or misleading, and that impression must be false or misleading in fact.

As was noted in *Chapter 1*, alleged cases of market manipulation that have been effected by the posting of bids and offers frequently boil down to whether such orders were 'genuine' and made in good faith. For example, in the regulatory action from 2014 involving an experienced bond dealer (see *Chapter 6*), the FCA accepted that:

> '[I]t was possible that other market participants could have traded with Mr [D] on the basis of his bids, and indeed this did on occasion happen. Its view is, however, that he did not intend that it should and in that sense the quotes were not genuine. It considers that Mr [D] deliberately bid in the smallest possible size in order to minimise the disadvantage to his trading book if this should happen.'[32]

---

32   FCA, *Final Notice*, 22 November 2017.

Of course, in criminal proceedings, the onus is on the prosecution to prove that the conduct was not genuine and so indicative of the requisite intention.

Section 91

Unlike sections 89 and 90 FSA 2012, section 91 had no direct predecessor. Rather, it evolved out of a major scandal in 2012, occasioned by the exposure of manipulation in the setting of LIBOR in the years after 2006.[33] During these years, traders were said to have made large profits for themselves and their employers by artificially raising and lowering the LIBOR rate by small fractions of a per cent in favour of their banks. Because very large sums were involved, even tiny changes in the rate could create significant profits or substantially limit losses.

Allegations that other financial benchmarks had been manipulated quickly followed. As a result, and following recommendations of a review of the regulation of LIBOR in September 2012,[34] the government decided to act. It introduced amendments to the Bill preceding the FSA 2012, so as to bring certain activities relating to the setting of financial benchmarks within its scope. This resulted in section 91 FSA 2012, which created new offences proscribing the manipulation of benchmark rates via the making of false or misleading statements or impressions.[35]

In order to understand how the section 91 offence operates, it is worth-while to examine the events leading to its drafting.

LIBOR and Other 'Relevant Benchmarks'

As its name suggests, the London Inter Bank Offered Rate is the interest rate which banks can charge each other on commercial loans in the London market. It has operated since 1986, although its roots can be traced

---

33 It has been suggested that extensive manipulation of LIBOR may also have gone on in the early 1990s: see Douglas Keenan, 'My Thwarted Attempt to Tell of Libor Shenanigans', *Financial Times*, 26 July 2012; https://www.ft.com/content/dc5f49c2-d67b-11e1-ba60-00144feabdco

34 See Martin Wheatley, *The Wheatley Review of LIBOR: Final Report* (2012); https://assets. publishing.service.gov.uk/government/uploads/system/uploads/attachment_data/file/191762/ wheatley_review_libor_finalreport_280912.pdf ('*Wheatley Review*').

35 Rider et al, *Market Abuse and Insider Dealing*, at 113.

back to the 1960s. In the years after 1986, LIBOR became a benchmark for many types of financial transaction around the world, including mortgages. By 2012, it was calculated across ten currencies and 15 borrowing periods, ranging from overnight to one year.[36] Thereafter, these were reduced to five currencies and seven maturities due to concerns that the low level of underlying trades in some rates could make them easier to manipulate.[37]

For every currency, a number of banks are selected, each of which are supposed to submit a rate which reflects market realities for the relevant period *without* reference to any other bank on the panel. The resulting submissions made by the various banks were, in the past, collated and averaged by British Bankers' Association LIBOR Ltd, an industry body. The top and bottom quartiles of submissions would typically be eliminated, and the average of the remainder then taken with a view to setting the promulgated rate. Even so, there was scope for manipulation by making artificial submissions to the benchmark administrator that could cause movement in the benchmark.

Once this manipulation came out into the open, the SFO took steps to investigate and prosecute. In the absence of an offence specifically addressing benchmark manipulation, the SFO was obliged to have recourse to the common law offence of conspiracy to defraud. Although most forms of common law conspiracy were abolished by section 5(1) of the Criminal Law Act 1977, conspiracy to defraud had been expressly preserved by section 5(2). As to its elements, the offence will be made out where there is an 'agreement by two or more people by dishonesty to deprive a person of something which is his or to which he is or would be entitled and an agreement by two or more by dishonesty to injure some proprietary right of his'.[38] The need for an agreement makes the offence more difficult to use against a single trader, although a conspiracy can be charged in connection with 'persons unknown' and it be left to inference from the facts that there must have been such a conspiracy. Dishonesty (discussed above) must also be present, but it is axiomatic that the offence is in the agreement to do something and so it is not necessary that the agreed outcome actually

---

36   Wheatley, *The Wheatley Review of LIBOR: Final Report*, at 1.1; 5.3.

37   Ibid; 'Libor', *Intercontinental Exchange* https://www.theice.com/iba/libor

38   *Scott v Metropolitan Police Commissioner* [1975] AC 819 at 840.

transpire. As such, conspiracy to defraud provided a vehicle for holding manipulators to account, but not an ideal one.

By way of illustration, in March 2019, two former Barclays' employees were convicted by majority verdict of conspiracy to defraud by submission of false rates between 2005 and 2009. This conviction followed their retrial at Southwark Crown Court. The two men had, in concert with traders at Deutsche Bank, acted with the intention of manipulating the Euro Inter Bank Offered Rate (EURIBOR), the European banks' equivalent of LIBOR. This would necessarily have been at the expense of others, not least because expert evidence suggests that up to US$180 trillion worth of financial products are linked to the rate.[39]

This trial brought to nine the number of people found guilty after six rate-rigging trials over the previous four years, starting with Tom Hayes' trial in 2015. This tranche of historic benchmark manipulation cases is, of course, coming to a close given the advent of section 91 FSA 2012.

Misleading Statements or Impressions in Relation to Benchmarks

Section 91 draws on sections 89 and 90 to create two new offences of manipulating financial benchmarks. By section 91(1) it is an offence for a person to make a false or misleading statement in the course of arrangements for the setting of a relevant benchmark, intending that the statement be used for setting that benchmark and knowing that it is false or misleading. This would include misleading submissions made to benchmark administrators but might extend considerably further. For example, it might include making deliberately inaccurate suggestions to 'panel banks' as to where a LIBOR rate would be set for a particular day.

Section 91(2) deals with misleading impressions. Specifically, the *actus reus* of the offence is the undertaking of an act or course of conduct 'which creates a false or misleading impression as to the price or value of any investment or as to the interest rate appropriate to any transaction'. However, the offence is committed only where the person intends to create the impression, and knows that or is reckless as to whether it is false or misleading,

---

39   Andy Verity, 'Former Barclays Traders Jailed over Euribor Rate-Rigging' *BBC News*, 1 April 2019; https://www.bbc.co.uk/news/business-47779993

as well as knowing that the impression may affect the setting of a relevant benchmark (which, in fact, it may).

CHAPTER 5

Criminal Defences and Punishment

Introduction

Even if the essential elements of one of the offences in Part 7 of the FSA 2012 are made out, an acquittal may yet be warranted by virtue of a defence. This chapter focusses on the crafted defences contained within Part 7, which are largely designed to prevent criminalisation of long-standing commercial practices considered legitimate and essential for the proper functioning of markets.

It bears noting that for each of the defences discussed, the legislation states that 'it is a defence for the person charged ... to show' (or similar). *Prima facie* this appears to place a legal burden on the defendant to prove them, albeit only on the balance of probabilities.[1] However, it seems more likely given the gravity of the offences (as reinforced by the penalties, below) that the accused is faced with only an evidential burden. The argument to this effect is based on the jurisprudence on the European Convention of Human Rights (ECHR) to the effect that a substantive legal burden is contrary to the right of an accused to a fair trial, and specifically the presumption of innocence.[2] Section 3 of the Human Rights Act 1998 then requires that the legal burden be 'read down', so that it becomes an evidential burden. This requires the accused simply to ensure the defence is raised on the evidence, from whichever party that derives. It is for the prosecution then to disprove the elements of the defence beyond reasonable doubt.[3]

---

1   *Carr-Briant* [1943] KB 607.

2   See *Lambert* [2001] UKHL 37; [2002] 2 AC 545.

3   Some complexities of this issue are discussed more fully in *The Little Book of Insider Dealing*.

The Statutory Defences

Section 89(3)

When it comes to prosecutions for making misleading statements under section 89(1) FSA 2012, section 89(3) provides that it will be a defence for the accused to 'show' that the statement was made in conformity with: (a) price stabilising rules; (b) control of information rules; or (c) the relevant EU provisions regarding exemptions for buy-back programmes or the stabilisation of financial instruments. These highly technical and specialist defences have been carried forward from section 397 FSMA, and refer to longstanding commercial practices. Examples may include the repurchasing of shares by the company that issued them as part of, for example, employee share option programmes, and the purchase of securities by an investment firm in the context of a significant distribution of those securities, to support their price for a predetermined period of time. As was noted in MAR (albeit in a regulatory context), these are considered legitimate for economic reasons.[4] Even so, their use is tightly controlled.

Section 90(9)

Section 90(9)(b)-(d) FSA 2012 created similar technical defences to the crime of making misleading impressions contrary to section 90(1) to those that are found in section 89(3) for making misleading statements (above). Thus, it would be a defence to show that the misleading impressions were made: to stabilise the price of investments, and in conformity with price stabilising rules; in conformity with control of information rules; or in conformity with approved exemptions for buy-back programmes and those for the stabilisation of financial instruments.

However, section 90(9)(a) also established a general defence to giving a 'misleading impression' in the circumstances specified in section 90(2); that is, where the defendant created the impression to induce another person to acquire, or dispose of investments etc. This defence provides that the accused is entitled to an acquittal if they can show that they 'reasonably

---

4   MAR, recital (11).

believed' their conduct would not create a false or misleading impression about the market in, or value of, relevant investments, albeit made with the intention of inducing another person to acquire or dispose of them etc. Thus, the accused would have to establish that they did so believe, and that it was reasonable to do so.

At first sight, this appears strange. Defences only become relevant if the prosecution has established all of the essential elements of its case. Thus, before the defence in section 90(9)(a) even needs to be considered, and pursuant to section 90(1)(a), the prosecution must have proved beyond reasonable doubt that the accused person 'intended to create' the false or misleading impression concerned. That being the case, how could the defendant establish that they did not believe their behaviour would create a false impression?

A dearth of case law means that a court has yet to explore this issue fully. However, it is possible to reconcile the provisions, if only on a theoretical basis. It might cover a situation where a defendant intended to give a specific impression, to induce another party into certain action, which impression turned out to be false, but which he or she reasonably believed would not be misleading when they (deliberately) gave such an impression. Nevertheless, the circumstances in which such a defence would become operative must be uncommon.

Section 91(3)-(4)

Unsurprisingly, the two offences relating to the manipulation of financial benchmarks created by section 91(1) and section 91(2) FSA 2012 — that is, respectively, false or misleading statements and false or misleading conduct affecting financial benchmarks — produce very similar technical defences to those found under section 89 and section 90. Thus, under section 91(3) it is a defence for the person charged under section 91(1) to show that a misleading statement was made in conformity with: price stabilising rules, control of information rules, or the relevant EU provisions regarding exemptions for buy-back programmes and the stabilisation of financial instruments. Similarly, in proceedings brought under section 91(2) it is a defence under section 91(4) for the defendant to show that they engaged in the misleading conduct to stabilise the price of investments and in conformity with price stabilising rules, or in conformity with control of information rules, or relevant EU provisions as regards exemptions for buy-back programmes and stabilisation of financial instruments.

Penalties

The penalties provision, section 92(1), makes it clear that each of the offences in Part 7 is triable either way. That means that they may either be tried summarily before the magistrates' court, if that is suitable and the defendant consents, or on indictment before a jury in the Crown Court otherwise.

As with all either-way offences, the maximum penalties differ depending on whether the trial is summary or on indictment. On summary trial, the maximum penalty is six months' imprisonment,[5] with or without a fine. On conviction in the Crown Court, the maximum is seven years' imprisonment, with or without a fine. In both cases, the maximum value of the fine is not limited.[6] Although no prosecutions under these provisions have yet been brought, it was suggested in 2015 that the maximum potential sentence be increased to ten years — the maximum available for conspiracy to defraud.[7]

Although primary legislation fixes maximum penalties, the Sentencing Council is a statutory body responsible for establishing, transparently and coherently, how courts should reach their sentencing decisions in any given case, via production of guidelines. However, there are currently no sentencing guidelines available for any of the offences under FSA 2012, nor FSMA before it. It may be argued that the fraud guideline, which addresses conspiracy to defraud, may be relevant, but it is more likely that the courts will conduct their own, independent exercise based on the statutory maximum,

---

5   This is the position in England and Wales, despite section 154(1) of the Criminal Justice Act 2003, which has not yet entered into force. Where the offence occurs in England and Wales after that date (should it occur), or in Scotland, the maximum term will be 12 months: section 92(2)(a)-(b).

6   See section 85 of the Legal Aid, Sentencing and Punishment of Offenders Act 2012, brought into force on 12 March 2015 by art 2 of the Legal Aid, Sentencing and Punishment of Offenders Act 2012 (Commencement No. 11) Order 2015.

7   See Fair and Effective Markets Review, *Final Report* (2015); https://www.bankofengland. co.uk/-/media/boe/files/report/2015/fair-and-effective-markets-review-final-report at 7, 12, 88–89.

previous decisions, and the facts of the individual case. The Sentencing Council has also published a General Guideline, with effect from October 2019, for use in the sentencing of offenders for which there is no offence specific guideline.[8]

The practical significance of various principles to date may be seen in sentences imposed for market abuse under predecessor statutes; for insider dealing under section 52 of the Criminal Justice Act 1993; and for broadly similar 'white-collar' offences.

For example, the Court of Appeal has emphasised the need for deterrence in market manipulation cases. In *Hayes* [2015] EWCA Crim 1944, [2018] 1 Cr App R 3 it noted that: '[T]his court must make clear to all in the financial and other markets in the City of London that conduct of this type, involving fraudulent manipulation of the markets, will result in severe sentences of considerable length'.[9] It may be said that deterrence is particularly necessary in relation to forms of criminality that are hard to detect but nonetheless have seriously damaging and widespread effects.

As with all offences, the defendant's level of culpability is particularly important. In light of the variants of each Part 7 offence, the defendant's state of mind will also be key to setting the appropriate penalty level. Thus, as confirmed by *Rigby and Bailey*, a crime committed recklessly is less serious than one perpetrated knowingly. It was also relevant in that case that the prison sentence was only part of their punishment. Rigby had been ordered to pay £840,000 in costs and compensation, while Bailey paid £142,000.[10] The court accepted that these financial penalties, as well as the stigma of the conviction and consequent loss of the ability to work in financial markets, should be taken into account.

As in any other case, sentences will be reduced where a guilty plea is

---

8   See Sentencing Council, *General Guideline: Overarching Principles;* https://
    www.sentencingcouncil.org.uk/overarching-guides/magistrates-court/item/
    general-guideline-overarching-principles/

9   At 109.

10 James Daley, 'Disgraced Former AIT Directors Forced to Pay £1m in Compensation and Legal
    Costs', *The Independent,* 21 December 2005; https://www.independent.co.uk/news/business/
    news/disgraced-former-ait-directors-forced-to-pay-163m-in-compensation-and-legal-
    costs-514933.html

entered.[11] There is a specific guideline from the Sentencing Council applicable to all offences,[12] according to which the maximum reduction available is one-third, where the plea is entered at the first hearing. After that, a sliding scale is introduced, with the maximum reduction for a guilty plea entered on the first day of trial being 10% and reducing even further, potentially to zero, for a plea that occurs during the course of those proceedings.

This can be quite significant in practice. For example, in July 2018, a sentence of five years' and four months' imprisonment was imposed on Christian Bittar for conspiring to rig interest rate benchmarks. Bittar also agreed to pay £3.3 million in costs and penalties. The sentencing judge noted that, although the fraud guideline indicated a starting point of seven years, the offence was so serious that a starting point of nine years was appropriate.[13] Personal mitigation reduced the sentence to eight years, and his guilty plea, despite its lateness, to five years and four months. That amounted to the maximum reduction of one-third, because the delay had been engendered by a genuine need for the Court of Appeal to clarify the law.[14]

11   See section 144 of the Criminal Justice Act 2003.

12   See Sentencing Council, *Reduction in Sentence for a Guilty Plea: Definitive Guideline*, 7 March 2017; https://www.sentencingcouncil.org.uk/publications/item/reduction-in-sentence-for-a-guilty-plea-definitive-guideline-2/

13   FCA, Final Notice: Christian Bittar, 14 September 2018; https://www.fca.org.uk/publication/final-notices/christian-bittar-2018.pdf at Appendix 2, 6.

14   Ibid at Appendix 2, 6–8.

CHAPTER 6

The Regulatory Regime and its Penalties

Introduction

The specific criminalisation of market manipulation by section 47(2) FSA 1986 initially appeared to be a success. Yet within a few years of the legislation coming into effect, informed observers were arguing that the criminal process did not operate effectively to deter manipulative conduct. The high standard of proof, use of juries, strict rules of evidence, and restrictively defined offences were often too demanding for prosecutors to satisfy. A new call therefore came for the criminal offences to be supplemented by a system of civil penalties.

Of course, it was already the case that lesser, and less clear-cut, cases of manipulation by finance industry professionals could sometimes be sanctioned by the exchanges on which they occurred. For example, in 1997, JP Morgan & Co was fined £350,000 by the LSE for a breach of its rules. Just before the index closed on 28 November 1997, two relatively small trades in the shares of pharmaceutical companies Glaxo Wellcome PLC and Smith-Kline Beecham PLC sent the stock exchange index into a sharp fall. The two traders had managed options contracts on the index and allegedly sold shares in the two stocks—important components of the index—with a view to driving it down. These allegations were never established before a court, but the company later also announced that two traders had been dismissed from its London office.[1]

Significantly, however, such informal sanctions by markets and employers were not available with respect to private traders. For this and other reasons,

---

1   'London Exchange Fines Morgan $577,000 in Manipulation Case', *New York Times*, 19 December 1997; https://www.nytimes.com/1997/12/19/business/london-exchange-fines-morgan-577000-in-manipulation-case.html

it was widely felt that they were no substitute for a regulatory regime capable of catching manipulative conduct falling through the cracks of the criminal law. It was hoped that the introduction of a non-criminal regime, covering a wider range of conduct, with a lower standard of proof for establishing wrongdoing, and not requiring a jury, would make it easier to punish, and so deter, market manipulation.

Such an analysis has not been confined to the UK. For example, France introduced administrative regulation of market abuse in 1989 to supplement its existing regime of criminal sanctions. In the UK, change duly occurred in December 2001, when the FSMA came into force. Section 397 FSMA replaced section 47 FSA 1986 with another criminal offence of market manipulation. However, at the same time, section 118 FSMA supplemented this provision by giving the newly established FSA the power to take regulatory action against market abuse, including manipulation. At the time, it was envisaged that criminal prosecutions would still be considered before any regulatory action was brought. Nonetheless, in practice it seems that the FSA spent much of its resources over the next few years testing out the new regulatory regime. That regime was slightly amended in 2005, in order to implement the provisions of the MAD.

After the financial crisis of 2007–2009, the focus on regulatory action waned somewhat in favour of renewed interest in criminal prosecutions. Nevertheless, regulatory actions are still brought on a fairly regular basis and, for market manipulation, regulatory proceedings are still slightly favoured on a numerical basis over criminal prosecutions.[2]

The once-innovative regulatory provisions of the FSMA were largely superseded by the entry into force of the new EU MAR on 3rd July 2016 (although much of the rest of the FSMA still remains intact). The effect of this regime, which remains current, is discussed in more detail below.

It bears noting that the regulator (currently the FCA) has brought all regulatory actions in this field. Although the position under the MAR is yet to be formally established, the High Court held in *Hall v Cable and Wireless PLC* [2009] EWHC 1793 (Comm) that there was no private right to bring

---

2   Karen Anderson, 'Focussing on Criminal Sanctions for Market Abuse' (2012) 7 *Journal of International Banking and Financial Law* 430.

an action under section 118 FSMA for market abuse. Such proceedings can in any case be lengthy and so unattractive to those who might seek to pursue them privately. For instance, in 2015–2016, an FCA regulatory case (of any type) took an average of 25.2 months to reach resolution by way of settlement. By 2017–18, this had increased to 32.3 months. However, if cases where the FCA made a final decision to take no further action are included in the total it fell from 25.7 months to 19.1 months over the same period.[3]

The MAR — Key Provisions

The regime established under the MAR has many similarities to that found under the FSMA, but there are also some important differences. In particular, the scope previously covered by the FSMA has been expanded to include new markets and financial instruments, while there have also been changes regarding permitted behaviours, such as the use of so-called safe harbours. The MAR also introduced a new regulatory offence of 'attempted market manipulation', allowing the inchoate offence to be punished in a regulatory context.

The key provision, however, is article 15, as interpreted in accordance with article 12 so as effectively to proscribe both transaction-based and information-based manipulation.

Article 15 MAR succinctly states: 'A person shall not engage in or attempt to engage in market manipulation'. Under article 12(1)(a), market manipulation comprises, *inter alia*, entering into a transaction, placing an order to trade, or any other behaviour which gives false or misleading signals as to the price, supply, or demand for a financial instrument or related spot commodity contract, or secures their price at an artificial level, *unless* the person entering into such activity establishes that it has been carried out for legitimate reasons, and conforms with an accepted market practice in accordance with article 13 (see below).

Article 12(2) then sets out a non-exhaustive list of behaviour that will be

---

3   See Chris Webber and Stephen Cole, 'FCA Caseload at Record Levels Despite Dropping More Cases Than Ever', *UK Finance Disputes and Regulatory Investigations Blog*, 28 September 2018; https://www.finance-disputes.co.uk/2018/09/fca-caseload-at-record-levels-despite-dropping-more-cases-than-ever/

considered to be market manipulation. This includes, inter alia: the buying or selling of financial instruments at the opening or closing of the market, which has or is likely to have the effect of misleading investors (article 12(2)(b)), and placing or cancelling orders on a trading venue by any means, which creates a false or misleading signal about the supply, demand or price of a financial instrument (article 12(2)(c)(iii)).

For the purposes of article 12(1)(c), market manipulation also comprises disseminating information through the media, including the Internet, or other means (such as face-to-face contacts), which gives or is likely to give false or misleading signals about the supply of, demand for or price of a financial instrument. This includes the dissemination of rumours, where the person who so acted knew or ought to have known that the information was false or misleading. For example, a person who knows the broker concerned has concocted his story would fall foul of this provision by reporting, 'I heard from a broker that PQR PLC is about to do X'. The provision covers a range of behaviour, from bogus statements about a company's prospects made in investment chatrooms on the web to untrue formal announcements via an RNS as to company profits.

Furthermore, under article 12(1)(d), such information-based manipulation extends to transmitting false or misleading information in relation to a financial benchmark, such as LIBOR (making it the equivalent of section 91 FSA 2012). Under article 12(2)(d), information-based manipulation includes taking advantage of access to traditional or electronic media to voice an opinion about a financial instrument, having previously taken positions on that instrument, and then profiting from the impact of the opinions voiced on its price, without having properly and publicly disclosed that conflict of interest. Thus, the fact that a statement is true, or that its maker believes it to be true, does not necessarily preclude market abuse in this situation (unlike the equivalent criminal provisions: see sections 89 and 91 FSA 2012).

As referred to above, article 13 deals with accepted market practices as an exception to the operation of article 15 over transaction-based conduct and is therefore extremely significant. Specifically, article 13(1) states:

'The prohibition in Article 15 shall not apply to the activities referred to in Article 12(1)(a), provided that the person entering into a transaction, placing an order to trade or engaging in any other behaviour establishes that such transaction, order or behaviour have been carried out for legitimate reasons, and conform with an accepted market practice as established in accordance with this Article.'

However, it is not sufficient for an individual simply to assert that their conduct constitutes 'an accepted market practice'; rather, that is for competent authorities to establish, taking into account six criteria. Nor can an accepted market practice be accepted at large. The relevant practice must be specifically accepted by the competent authority of each individual market to which it is said to apply. A competent authority must notify ESMA and other competent authorities at least three months before an accepted market practice is intended to take effect.[4] Such practices are not then set in stone, but rather must be reviewed and monitored over time by both competent authorities and ESMA.[5]

'Relevant Investments'

Regulatory market abuse offences under MAR do not apply to all financial instruments, but only to those of a kind specified in Article 2. In general terms, under article 2(1)(a)-(c), they cover financial instruments admitted to trading on a regulated market, an MTF, or an organised trading facility (OTF). However, it also applies to derivative financial instruments which do not fall into one of these categories, but the 'price or value of which depends on or has an effect on the price or value of a financial instrument referred to in those points …': article 2(1)(d).

Article 4 MAR requires that ESMA publish a consolidated list of financial instruments that are traded on EU venues, having received that information from each Member State's regulator. This list is maintained as a searchable database on ESMA's website,[6] via which any market participant may

---

4   See article 13(2).

5   See article 13(8), (10).

6   See https://registers.esma.europa.eu/publication/searchRegister?core=esma_registers_firds

establish whether an instrument is within MAR's scope.

Under the pre-MAR regulatory system, some consideration was given to the extent of this list and, more pertinently, the meaning of 'related' investments. Section 130A FSMA permitted the Treasury to specify 'qualifying investments' for the purpose of the regulatory offences under that Act. 'Related investments' — that is, 'in relation to a qualifying investment, … an investment whose price or value depends on the price or value of the qualifying investment'[7] — were also within the remit of the regulatory offences on insider dealing.

This definition, which is substantially the same as that now contained in article 2(1)(d) MAR, was considered in *Canada Inc v FCA* [2013] EWCA Civ 1662. In that case, the FCA alleged that a Canadian company named Swift Trade Inc (Swift) had engaged in manipulative trading of shares on the LSE, in violation of section 118(5) FSMA. It was claimed that in the year after 1 January 2007, Swift deliberately filed false orders with Merrill Lynch & Penson (MLP) by way of CFDs for shares quoted on the LSE. The alleged purpose was to manipulate the price of individual securities. Once the orders were placed, MLP automatically hedged those orders via a computer system by placing orders of their own to buy or sell an equivalent quantity of the shares ordered. The dealers would then cancel the original orders being placed, and the consequent hedging orders were also automatically cancelled. However, in the meantime, there would have been a movement in the price of the shares. Swift profited by buying or selling those securities at the new, manipulated price, eventually netting the firm in excess of £1.75m.

Swift's defence was, in part, that it had not engaged in manipulative behaviour under the FSMA because it had been involved with CFDs. It was said that, unlike shares, CFDs were not qualifying investments for the purposes of the FSMA. This argument was rejected at first instance by the UT(TCC) and then also on appeal. The Court of Appeal concluded that, even if Swift did not effect transactions or orders to trade in qualifying investments (because CFDs did not have this status), its behaviour nevertheless

---

7   Section 130A(3) of the FSMA (now repealed).

occurred 'in relation to' such investments. This was for the simple reason that the CFDs were made in relation to specific shares, which were, of course, qualifying investments. The court noted that the words 'in relation to' were of great width and were deliberately used in the statute for that very reason. The same view may well be taken of article 2(1)(d), although that of course is piece of EU, rather than UK, legislation.

Despite the broad manner in which these words are defined, investments are not within the MAR unless they fall within its definitions. For example, the degree to which cryptocurrencies such as Bitcoin were within its scope was until recently entirely open to question, despite their analogy to some regulated financial instruments.[8] This lack of clarity led the ESMA in January 2019 to publish an Advice analysing the position.[9] The FCA has also recently circulated its new Guidance on Cryptoassets[10] explaining how these fall within the agency's regulatory remit, including in connection with the MAR. It seems that the only general answer is that one cannot generalise and must consider the characteristics of the relevant crypto-asset to see if it meets the definition of a financial instrument within the meaning of article 2.

It also bears noting that the relevant financial instrument must have a connection as specified in article 2 with a regulated market, MTF or OTF. Nonetheless, the relevant transaction, order or behaviour leading to an allegation of market manipulation need not itself take place on a trading venue.

Territoriality

The MAR, as applicable within the UK, applies to conduct taking place not only within the country's borders but beyond it. As Anderson and Vance explain, through the MAR's extraterritorial effect, 'market manipulation

---

8   See e.g. Alexander Snyers and Karl Pauwels, 'ICOs in Belgium: Down the Rabbit Hole into Legal No Man's Land? Part 1' (2018) 29(8) *International Company and Commercial Law Review* 483–510 at 505–506; Nik Yeo and Joseph Farmer, 'Mapping the Landscape: Cryptocurrency Disputes under English Law: Part 2' (2019) 5 *Journal of International Banking and Financial Law* 290 at 292–93.

9   See ESMA, *Advice: Initial Coin Offerings and Crypto-Assets* (2019) ESMA50–157–1391; https://www.esma.europa.eu/sites/default/files/library/esma50-157-1391_crypto_advice.pdf

10 See FCA, *Guidance on Cryptoassets: Feedback and Final Guidance to CP 19/3* (2019) Policy Statement PS19/22; https://www.fca.org.uk/publication/policy/ps19-22.pdf

conducted from another country will be caught by the UK regime if the misleading impression or market distortion that it creates impacts on the UK'.[11] In this respect, the MAR is similar to the current criminal regime.

Extra-territoriality is not a new feature of market manipulation within the UK, as shown by the earlier example of the case against the Dubai-based investor pursued by the FSAu. Similarly, in 2013, the FCA took enforcement action against a US-based individual, trading through a direct market access provider, for 'layering' by using an algorithmic programme to place thousands of orders on the ICE Futures Europe exchange in the UK.[12]

Enforcement

The FCA can take non-criminal regulatory action against market abuse through two separate avenues. By far the most important is the 'enforcement action' under section 123 FSMA, by which the FCA can pursue market abuse through its own regulatory enforcement process and Regulatory Decisions Committee (RDC).

Alternatively, and quite exceptionally, the FCA may effectively seek a statutory injunction against a person under section 381 FSMA, restraining violation of article 15 MAR that either is already occurring or has a 'reasonable likelihood' of doing so. An application for such an order must be made to the High Court (in England and Wales).[13] Moreover, the FCA can also apply to the court requesting that it consider imposing an 'administrative sanction'.[14] The available sanctions are: a financial penalty, payable to the FCA 'of such amount as the court considers appropriate'; suspension of authorisation or restriction of conduct; or, if the person concerned is an individual (rather than a corporate entity), a temporary or permanent

---

11   See Karen Anderson and Eleanor Vance, 'When Does the Market Abuse Regime Apply?', in Anderson et al, *A Practitioner's Guide*, at 2–001.

12   Austin, *Insider Trading and Market Manipulation: Investigating and Prosecuting Across Borders*, at 168.

13   In Scotland, the application is made to the Court of Sessions, seeking an interdict prohibiting the contravention.

14   See section 129 of the FSMA.

prohibition on certain investment-related activities.[15]

The High Court is not bound by the complex scheme for assessing penalties drawn up by the FCA and set out in Part 6 of the FCA's *Handbook*.[16] Nonetheless, in *Da Vinci Invest*, the High Court indicated that these criteria would be treated as its starting point, if only to avoid a divergence in treatment of such cases dependent only upon the route taken.

Notwithstanding the availability of court-based sanctions, however, the vast majority of non-criminal actions for market manipulation go through the 'normal' regulatory route, considered next.

Procedure for an Enforcement Action

If, following an initial investigation, the Enforcement and Market Oversight Division (EMOD or Enforcement) of the FCA believe that there is a case to answer their investigative teams will often conduct a preliminary meeting with the subject. These interviews provide an opportunity for investigators to set out their case theory in general terms.[17] Discussions on a 'without prejudice' basis may be held, based on a draft formal notice setting out the regulator's view of the facts, the alleged breaches, and the proposed penalties.[18] These negotiations may lead to a full settlement of the action, although constraints of time mean that the FCA will continue to prepare their case in parallel, in case an agreement is not reached. Such settlements are always made on the basis of an admission of liability.[19]

In March 2017 the FCA introduced focused resolution agreements (FRAs) to allow those being investigated to contest part of any proposed

---

15 Where the prohibition is permanent it may concern only the individual's involvement in the management of an investment firm. Where the prohibition is temporary, it may alternatively address the individual's acquisition or disposal of financial instruments, or bidding on certain platforms, whether done for themselves or others: see section 129(7) of the FSMA.

16 Part 6 is specifically designated as the *Decision Procedure and Penalties Manual* (DEPP).

17 HM Treasury, *Review of Enforcement Decision-making at the Financial Services Regulators: Final Report* (2014) at 28; https://assets.publishing.service.gov.uk/government/uploads/system/uploads/attachment_data/file/389063/enforcement_review_response_final.pdf

18 McMullen and Proudlock, 'United Kingdom: Financial Services Enforcement and Investigation', at 52–59.

19 See generally the helpful flowchart set out within the FCA's *Enforcement Information Guide* (2017) at 5–6 https://www.fca.org.uk/publication/corporate/enforcement-information-guide.pdf

enforcement action before the RDC while retaining at least some of the early settlement discount to which they would otherwise have been entitled for making admissions. Where the maker of an FRA successfully challenges the FCA's characterisation of misconduct, the early settlement discount will range between 15% and 30%. Challenges only to the proposed penalty will still enjoy a full 30% early settlement discount.[20]

If a full settlement is not reached, the matter, or whatever part of it has not been agreed under an FRA, will have to go before the RDC. The EMOD will prepare and submit to the RDC the case papers, including an investigation report, preliminary findings, and a suggested penalty.[21] Although the RDC is part of the FCA, and its panel members are appointed by and accountable to the FCA's board, it is operationally entirely distinct.[22] Its separation has also been considerably enhanced in recent years. Those members of the FCA who were involved in the initial investigation will have no involvement in the RDC's decision-making process.[23] Apart from its chairman, none of the members of the RDC is an FCA employee. The RDC also has its own legal advisers and secretariat, distinct from those recommending any action.[24]

Normally, a panel of three people will sit on the RDC to consider a contested case. This is usually made up of a presiding chair or deputy chair, drawn from a pool of experienced professional lawyers, and two lay members, usually drawn from business, consumer, or finance industry backgrounds.[25] Each member of the RDC panel is entitled to vote on the matter under consideration, although the presiding member will have the casting vote in a tie where the panel is comprised of an even number of members (unusual).[26] Nevertheless, it is the final stage of an administrative decision-making process, not a judicial hearing; the RDC is not a tribunal.[27]

---

20 See DEPP 5.1.1, 6.7.3A.
21 *Enforcement Information Guide* (2017) at 6.
22 The RDC is not a creature of statute; its constitution and procedure are contained in DEPP 3 of the FCA's *Handbook*.
23 Rider et al, *Market Abuse and Insider Dealing*, at 294.
24 DEPP 3.1.3.
25 DEPP 3.2.2.
26 DEPP 3.2.8.
27 DEPP 3.2.11.

It must follow the procedure described in DEPP 3.2, but subject to that, may conduct itself in whatever way the presiding member considers suitable to determine a matter fairly and expeditiously.[28]

If, after reviewing the papers and findings of the initial investigation, the RDC decides action is appropriate, it will issue a warning notice to the person or firm under investigation.[29] This forms part of the FSMA's framework involving warning, decision, discontinuance, and final notices. The warning notice must state the amount of any financial penalty that the RDC is initially minded to impose and, if the decision is to suspend or restrict the recipient's performance of a regulated function, the intended duration of this. The proposed terms of any statement censuring the dealer that is intended to be published must also be set out.[30]

The recipient of the notice may then make written or oral representations on its contents to the RDC. If oral, a representations meeting is arranged between the subject of the investigation, their lawyers (if instructed) and the RDC. This allows suspects to advance arguments against the FCA taking any action at all, and about the penalty that should be imposed if it does. Normally, the FCA's Enforcement team, the RDC's legal advisers, and a case handler from its secretariat will also be present.[31]

In the post-representation stage, the RDC will decide whether it is appropriate to issue the decision notice containing the enforcement action initially proposed.[32] If, after reviewing a matter, the RDC decides that action is not appropriate, it will inform the parties and relevant FCA staff, such that a notice of discontinuance may thereafter be issued.[33] By contrast, if action is deemed to be the correct course, or is agreed upon as part of a settlement, the RDC will issue a decision notice.[34] This will contain details of the proposed penalties, whether fines, suspensions from regulated activities, public

---

28 See DEPP 3.2.8.

29 *Enforcement Information Guide* at 6.

30 See section 126 FSMA.

31 See FCA, *Regulatory Decisions Committee (RDC)*, 6 September 2019; https://www.fca.org.uk/about/committees/regulatory-decisions-committee-rdc

32 See DEPP 3.2.23.

33 See DEPP 3.2.25–26.

34 See DEPP 3.2.27 and DEPP 5.1.1.

censures, or a combination of the three.[35]

Significantly more cases end by a formal agreement being made between the RDC and the alleged market abuser than by the RDC making a unilateral decision. Nonetheless, in very general terms, individuals appear more likely to challenge proposed penalties, while companies show greater inclination to settle.[36]

If an adverse decision notice is issued by the RDC without agreement, the person subject to it has the right to refer the matter to the UT(TCC) within 28 days of receiving it, as the decision notice must make clear.

In the absence of such a reference, the FCA will issue a final notice containing details of the enforcement action to be taken.[37] If the person investigated fails to pay any financial penalty contained in a final notice, the FCA can recover the amount due as a debt owed, like any other civil debt[38] (although of course this poses problems where the person is, or becomes, impecunious).

Reference to the Upper Tribunal

After a decision notice has been issued by the RDC, the person to whom it is addressed may refer the matter to the UT(TCC) if the decision notice involves imposition of a penalty, prohibition, suspension or restriction, or publication of a statement of censure.[39] (Alternatively, under the FCA's expedited reference procedure, the subject of an investigation can elect not to engage in the RDC stage and go directly to the UT(TCC).)[40]

To proceed on a reference following a decision notice, the applicant must send or deliver a signed reference notice to the UT(TCC), to be received there no later than 28 days after notice was given of the decision regarding which the reference is made. Certain details must also be included, along

---

35 See section 127 FSMA.

36 Caroline Binham, 'Rise in Disputes over UK Financial Watchdog Penalties', *Financial Times*, 11 February 2018; https://www.ft.com/content/570b2cc2-0d99-11e8-839d-41ca06376bf2

37 See section 390 FSMA; *Enforcement Information Guide* at 6; DEPP 5.1.8.

38 Michael Filby, 'The Enforcement of Insider Dealing under the Financial Services and Markets Act 2000' (2003) 24(11) *Company Lawyer* 334–41 at 334.

39 See section 127(d) FSMA.

40 See DEPP 5.1.8E–5.1.8J; see also 3.2.22A.

with a copy of the notice of the decision.[41] The FCA must also be sent a copy of the reference notice at the same time.[42] Normally, the UT(TCC) must then enter the details of the applicant's reference notice into its register of references and decisions in financial services cases, and notify the applicant and the FCA when it has done so.[43]

The FCA must send or deliver a 'statement of case' (that is, a written statement) explaining its decision, to be received no more than 28 days after the FCA receives the UT(TCC)'s notification.[44] Finally, the applicant must submit to the UT(TCC) and the FCA, in writing, an explanation of those elements of the statement that are disputed and why, to be received by the UT(TCC) no more than 28 days after the applicant received the FCA's statement of case.[45] The matter will then be set down for a final hearing, although there may also be a preliminary hearing beforehand if there is some complexity requiring that further steps be taken.[46]

In London, the UT(TCC) sits in the Rolls Building in Fetter Lane. Oral hearings may also take place in Manchester or Edinburgh, or exceptionally, in other court centres if a party is unable to travel.[47] The hearing is not an appeal but, instead, the first judicial (rather than administrative) examination of the matter, which it considers entirely *de novo*. As a result, neither party has to show that the RDC has erred in any way in reaching its decision.[48]

Under section 133(4) FSMA, the UT may consider any evidence that is

---

41 As to procedure on reference to the Upper Tribunal, see rule 26B and Schedule 3 of the Tribunal Procedure (Upper Tribunal) Rules 2008, noting that the definition of a 'financial service case' includes a reference to the UT in respect of a decision of the FCA (rule 1(3)). See also HM Courts and Tribunals Service, *Making a Reference to the Upper Tribunal (Tax and Chancery Chamber)* (2014) ('*Making a Reference*'); https://assets.publishing.service.gov.uk/government/uploads/system/uploads/attachment_data/file/716231/t400-eng.pdf

42 See Tribunal Procedure (Upper Tribunal) Rules 2008, rule 1(3) (definition of 'respondent' (da)) and Schedule 3, para 2(5).

43 See Tribunal Procedure (Upper Tribunal) Rules 2008, Schedule 3, para 3.

44 Ibid para 4.

45 Ibid para 5.

46 *Making a Reference* at 6.

47 See *Making a Reference* at 6.

48 See the general explanation of the process in practice by David Mayhew, *Financial Services Regulation: Challenge in The Upper Tribunal* (2012, ThirtyNine Essex Street; http://www.39essex.com/docs/articles/challenge_in_the_tribunal_-_dm.pdf

relevant to the subject matter of the reference. This is so whether or not the evidence was available when the RDC made its earlier decision, such that entirely new material may be adduced by each party. However, as noted in 2005 by the UT(TCC)'s predecessor, the Financial Services and Markets Tribunal (FSMT): 'As a matter of common sense and fairness we would generally expect the FSA with the wide powers open to it, having taken time to evaluate matters, and having carefully reviewed and carried forward charges to the RDC, to bring much the same case when taken to this Tribunal'.[49]

Risks in Going to the Upper Tribunal

Before the Upper Tribunal, both the FCA and the applicant may argue that the outcome should differ from that reached by the RDC. Given that the FCA's case would generally be expected to be the same as before the RDC and that only the person subject to the decision notice has a right of reference, this is likely to be rare. Nonetheless, an example of this occurred in early 2006. The RDC decided that a senior hedge fund trader had engaged in market abuse contrary to section 118 FSMA by short-selling $16 million worth of shares in Sumitomo Mitsui Financial Group. The RDC therefore fined him £750,000.

Although this was, at the time, the largest regulatory fine the FSAu had issued against an individual, it was still less than the £1,000,000 that the FSAu's Enforcement Division had originally sought. More significantly, the RDC did not make any finding that the trader's conduct was in breach of PRIN 2.1.1(1) (the principle of integrity) to such a degree that he was not a fit person to carry on regulated business. The RDC therefore did not conclude that his authorisation should be withdrawn.[50]

The trader initially referred the RDC's decision to fine him to the FSMT. In response, in its statement of case, the FSAu sought to re-introduce the issues of integrity and withdrawal of authorisation. A preliminary question for the FSMT was whether the FSAu could ask it to reconsider matters that its own RDC had already rejected. The tribunal concluded that the subject matter of the referral entailed all the circumstances, evidence, and allegations

---

49 *Legal & General Assurance Society v FSAu* [2005] FSMT 015 at 15.
50 See *Trader's Name v FSAu* [2002] UKFSM FSM035 at 12.

that had gone before the RDC, and not just its eventual decision. As all the matters that would be relied on by the FSAu before the FSMT had previously been raised before the RDC, the FSMT held that the regulator *could* re-introduce the issue of integrity and withdrawal of authorisation at a substantive hearing.[51] Following this decision, the trader withdrew his reference to the FSMT, so that in August 2006, the FSAu duly published a final notice imposing the original penalty of £750,000.[52]

The decision reached in this case was confirmed in 2008. In that case, the RDC found that an individual had acted recklessly, simply closing his mind to the risk that his preferences would be used to influence LIBOR submissions to the benefit of his trading positions. The EMOD did not accept the RDC's finding, asserting instead that the individual acted dishonestly and in the knowledge that his conduct was improper. In that context, the UT(TCC) observed that: 'It is well-established that it is open to the Authority to pursue before the Tribunal an issue that was rejected by the RDC provided, as is the case here, the issue falls within the scope of the matter referred'. However, in the instant case, no dishonesty was found.[53]

In light of these decisions, parties considering whether to refer a matter to the UT(TCC) should appreciate that all aspects of the case before the RDC might be at large at the hearing. How far this extends is slightly uncertain. For example, had the senior hedge fund trader (see above) merely been fined £750,000, but the FSAu's Enforcement Division never sought withdrawal of authorisation, could the regulator have asked that the £1,000,000 fine they had originally requested be imposed by the Tribunal? (The present authors suggest that they could.) Of course, if an applicant has been wholly unsuccessful before the RDC, there will be few risks. In contrast, where the applicant has enjoyed mixed fortunes, winning on some issues and losing on others, a degree of caution might be prudent before proceeding further.

---

51   Ibid at 27–38.

52   FSAu, *Final Notice*, 1 August 2006.

53   *Trader's Name v FCA* [2018].

The Tribunal Hearing

The UT(TCC) is a superior court of record, such that its decisions have value as precedent.[54] Typically, it will have a bench comprising a judge and one or two non-legal members, who will often have special expertise in financial matters. A judge may, however, sit without any non-legal members where a significant point of law arises.[55] Whilst some judges hold full-time salaried positions, most serve on a part-time, fee-paid, basis. Nonetheless, all judges are independent of and unconnected to the FCA.[56]

Proceedings before the UT(TCC) are normally held in public. Cases can last from a few hours to several consecutive days, while unusually complex cases have been known to extend over a number of weeks. Like most tribunals, the UT(TCC) is not bound by the strict rules of evidence.[57] The parties must exchange lists of documents they intend to rely on when sending their respective statement of case and written reply well in advance of the oral hearing.[58] Much evidence is given by means of written statements, but witnesses may be called live as well.[59] A transcript of the proceedings before the RDC will usually be available to the UT(TCC) as well.

Illustrative cases demonstrate the flexibility of the UT(TCC)'s processes. *Geddis v FSAu* [2011] UKUT 344 (TCC) involved alleged manipulation on the London Metal Exchange (LME). The evidence comprised documentation; recordings and transcripts of relevant (preserved) conversations and FSAu interviews; witness statements; and live evidence from an expert concerning trading on the LME. The appellant also adduced seven favourable character witness statements. In *Hussein v FCA* [2018] UKUT 186 (TCC) the FCA called no live witnesses of fact but relied entirely on documentary evidence. In particular, it placed reliance on its interpretation of 21 recorded-electronic discussions that took place on UBS's internal systems between trader-submitters in early 2009.

After hearing from both sides, the UT(TCC) usually reserves its decision,

---

54   See section 3(5) of the Tribunals, Courts and Enforcement Act 2007 ('TCEA').

55   See *Making a Reference* at 7.

56   See section 3 and Schedule 14, Part 3, of the Constitutional Reform Act 2005.

57   See generally Tribunal Procedure (Upper Tribunal) Rules 2008, rule 15.

58   See Tribunal Procedure (Upper Tribunal) Rules 2008, Schedule 3, paragraphs 4(3) and 5(3).

59   Ibid rule 15.

which is conveyed to the parties within three months. If a party considers that the decision contains an error of law, the aggrieved party may seek leave to appeal to the Court of Appeal. The application for leave must in the first instance be made to the UT(TCC) itself; if that is refused, the aggrieved party may again seek leave from the Court of Appeal.[60]

Penalties

Section 123 FSMA allows the FCA to impose a penalty upon those who contravene article 15 MAR. These can be severe, as section 123 allows the regulator to impose 'a penalty of such amount as it considers appropriate', without limit. As a result, regulatory fines can include very significant punitive elements, often far more than any disgorgement of profits made by wrongdoing. Penalties are then paid over to the Exchequer, apart from certain enforcement costs that are retained by the FCA.[61]

As already noted, the FCA also has the power to prohibit a person from conducting certain regulated activities, or to suspend or restrict their permission to do so, for breach of article 15 MAR. The FCA may also publicly censure a person for such contravention, which alone could have career-ending implications.[62]

It is not only those working in the finance industry but also private traders who can be dealt with in this manner, albeit that the latter may have less to fear from a ban on conducting regulated activity. For example, in 2011, the FSAu fined a trader working from home £700,000 for manipulative trading in the shares of Domino Printing Sciences PLC on the LSE, contrary to section 118(5)(a) and (b) FSMA. The trader was also ordered to pay £322,818 in restitution to firms that had suffered losses as a result of his actions. He was also banned from working in a regulated finance industry for five years, pursuant to the general power in section 56 FSMA to prohibit persons who are not fit and proper.[63]

As to the determination of what penalties are appropriate in cases proved

---

60   Section 13(4)-(5) TCEA.

61   See FCA, *Enforcement*, 24 April 2019; https://www.fca.org.uk/about/enforcement

62   See sections 123–123C FSMA.

63   FSAu, *Final Notice*, 14 June 2011.

by the regulatory route, a five-step structured penalties regime was introduced by the FSAu in March 2010. This is now set out at DEPP 6.5 and is based on three principles: disgorgement, discipline, and deterrence. These principles respectively mean that a firm or individual should not benefit from any breach; should be penalised for wrongdoing; and should be deterred (along with others) from further breaches. The five-step process helps to determine the punitive level of any financial penalty imposed, and makes allowance for early admissions and settlement by the person investigated, as well for as extreme impecuniosity on their part, and other mitigating and aggravating factors.

The process set out in DEPP 6.5 was first used in May 2011, when the FSAu dealt with a serious case of wash trading by a stock market trader. The FSAu ordered disgorgement of £210,563 (Step 1) and a disciplinary sum of £884,365 (Step 2), leading to a total financial penalty of £1,094,900 (after rounding down). The trader had qualified for a reduction of 30% on the disciplinary sum (not, of course, the disgorgement) under the FSAu's early settlement discount scheme. Without the discount, the disciplinary element of the financial penalty would have been £1,263,379. The FSAu also obtained a High Court injunction restraining the trader from committing further market abuse. In setting the level of the penalty, it appears that the FSAu was influenced by the defendant's alleged but unproven misconduct in the market on an earlier occasion.[64]

Similarly, in May 2011, a director of SP Bell, was fined and banned from working in financial services for his role in the FEI share ramping scheme (see below). The UT(TCC) determined that the appropriate financial penalty would have been significantly higher than the £25,000 imposed but for the director's poor financial position: a larger penalty would have forced him into bankruptcy.[65] Likewise, in 2014, the FCA fined Martin Brokers (UK) Ltd £630,000 for misconduct relating to setting LIBOR. The company had qualified for the early settlement discount of 30% discount, without

---

64   See report in Mischon de Reya, *Enforcement Watch: Issue 4;* https://www.mishcon.com/assets/managed/docs/downloads/doc_2499/EF4.pdf The final notice in this case is no longer available via the FSAu's archived website.

65   See *Trader's Name v FSAu* [2011] UKUT B36 (TCC).

which, the fine would have been £900,000. However, this was itself a major reduction from the £3,600,000 that the company would have been fined but for the fact that it was able to show that it could not pay such a sum in addition to the other regulatory fines that it faced.[66]

It has been suggested by some informed observers that the considerations employed by the FCA when reaching the penalties outlined in its final notices are sometimes rather opaque. There is little clarity as to precisely how aggravating and mitigating factors are assessed, or the role of deterrence in greatly increasing the penalty imposed.[67]

The potential advantages gained from co-operating with the FCA may encourage those accused of manipulation to accept the regulator's interpretation of the law in circumstances that are not absolutely clear-cut. In 2011, a private investor said that he had only agreed to settle his case with the FSAu because his lawyers had advised him that it was in his best interests to do so. His fine of £700,000 could have been £1 million but for the settlement discount. He nonetheless believed that he would have won if he had decided to contest the matter and been willing to take it to the UT(TCC).[68]

Illustrative Cases

The two cases outlined below provide examples of the two main forms of manipulation, namely misleading conduct and false statements, dealt with by way of regulatory action.

Winterflood

In 2010, the FSAu commenced regulatory proceedings against the chief executive (CE) of brokerage and fund management firm S P Bell, alleging that he had operated a share-ramping scheme. This scheme was aimed at raising the price of Fundamental-E Investments (FEI), a technology

---

66 FCA, *Final Notice: Martin Brokers (UK) Ltd*, 15 May 2014; https://www.fca.org.uk/publication/final-notices/martin-brokers-uk-ltd.pdf

67 Clare McMullen and Elly Proudlock, 'United Kingdom: Financial Services Enforcement and Investigation', in Marieke Breijer (ed.), *The European, Middle Eastern and African Investigations Review 2018* (2018, Global Investigations Review) 56–60 at 52–59.

68 See Jill Treanor, 'Trader Who is Barred from City Aims to Teach His Secrets', *The Guardian*, 14 June 2011; https://www.theguardian.com/business/2011/jun/14/trader-banned-market-abuse

company listed on the LSE's AIM, to an artificially high level. The CE was the chairman of FEI and had also acquired 85% of the shares in the company. Between July 2003 and July 2004, he instructed S P Bell employees to buy and sell shares in FEI for clients, many of whom, it was alleged, were unaware that their accounts were being used for this purpose. He also used brokers at Winterflood Securities to execute some of these trades. FEI's shares increased from 2.5p to 11.75p, tripling in value in the four months before the FSAu announced its investigation in July 2004. FEI's shares were then suspended from dealing and later crashed, losing many investors large amounts of money.

The CE admitted some of the allegations, but vehemently denied that his aim was to drive up the company's share price, rather than to 'park the shares' in the clients' accounts while he planned a takeover of FEI. Even so, the FSAu concluded that his behaviour amounted to market abuse contrary to sections 118(2)(b) and (c) FSMA.[69] The FEI shares constituted qualifying investments, which were traded on AIM — a prescribed market — while his conduct was likely to give a regular user of that market a false or misleading impression as to the demand for, and value of, FEI shares.

The FSAu also found against Winterflood and two of its traders. It should be stressed that there was no allegation that they had deliberately committed any regulatory offence. The CE himself subsequently stated that he was: 'astonished they [Winterflood] have been fined as it was not possible they could have known what was happening and, as far as they were concerned, no rules were being broken'.[70]

However, as already noted, in a regulatory context, market abuse can be found without any intent being present. Margaret Cole, then Director of Enforcement at the FSAu, observed that: 'Winterflood allowed highly profitable trades to go ahead despite clear warnings that something was amiss. Their actions led to serious losses for investors and damaged market

---

69   See now articles 12 and 15 MAR.

70   Simon Watkins, 'FSA Hands Out Record £2.8m Fine to [E] over Share Ramping', *Mail on Sunday*, 2 May 2010.

confidence'.[71]

In consequence of the findings, the CE was fined £2.8m pursuant to section 123(3) FSMA. This was made up of £1.3 million representing disgorgement of profits and an additional £1.5 million disciplinary component for what the FSAu described as a 'complex and prolonged abusive scheme'. He was also banned for life from working in the financial services industry pursuant to section 56 FSMA.[72] Winterflood Securities was fined £4 million, including £900,000 in disgorgement of profits, while two of its traders were personally fined £200,000 and £50,000 respectively.[73]

Tesco

In March 2017, the FCA found that Tesco PLC and Tesco Stores Limited (Tesco Stores) were in violation of section 118(7) FSMA[74] by disseminating information that gave a false or misleading impression regarding shares in the companies, which they knew or ought reasonably to have known was false or misleading.[75]

In essence, Tesco PLC published a trading update on 29 August 2014 in which it stated that it expected profits for the six-month period ending on 23 August to be in the region of £1.1 billion. However, almost a month later, on 22 September 2014, the company published a corrective trading update in which it announced that it had identified a significant 'overstatement' of its expected profit for the half-year in the earlier announcement, prompting a fall in share price. (They had, *inter alia*, 'pulled forward' income from subsequent reporting periods). As a result, purchasers of shares and bonds in the company during the weeks between these two announcements paid

---

71 Harry Wilson, 'Winterflood Loses Final Appeal against £4m Market Abuse Fine', *The Telegraph*, 23 April 2010; https://www.telegraph.co.uk/finance/newsbysector/banksandfinance/7621019/Winterflood-loses-final-appeal-against-4m-market-abuse-fine.html

72 FSAu, *Final Notice*, 18 May 2010.

73 Wilson, 'Winterflood Loses Final Appeal against £4m Market Abuse Fine', *The Telegraph*, 23 April 2010; https://www.telegraph.co.uk/finance/newsbysector/banksandfinance/7621019/Winterflood-loses-final-appeal-against-4m-market-abuse-fine.html; FSAu, *Final Notice*, 18 May 2010.

74 See now articles 12 and 15 MAR.

75 Much of the content in this case study is drawn from 'Tesco to Compensate Investors after Admitting Market Abuse' (2017) 38(7) *Company Lawyer* 215–16.

a higher price than would otherwise have been the case, as the company appeared to be doing better than was actually the situation.

The FCA did not suggest that Tesco PLC's board of directors knew of the false and misleading nature of the August statement. However, it found that there was knowledge at a sufficiently high level for it to constitute the knowledge of Tesco PLC for the purposes of market abuse. It was not necessary that the dissemination be committed by the 'directing mind and will' of the company.

Tesco admitted liability and agreed to pay compensation to up to 10,000 retail and institutional investors who had purchased shares and bonds on or after the 29 August 2014 and who still held those securities when the statement was corrected on 22 September 2014. This was the first time the FCA used its (extant) powers under section 384(5) FSMA to require a listed company to pay restitution for market abuse in accordance with such arrangements as the regulator considered 'appropriate'. Those amounts were, however, to be determined with the assistance of an independent expert engaged by the FCA. The total amount of restitution potentially payable was assessed at about £85 million (plus interest). The restitution scheme would be administered on Tesco's behalf by KPMG.

In consequence of the companies' acceptance of responsibility and agreement to the restitution order, as well as Tesco Stores' entry into a deferred prosecution agreement (DPA)[76] with the SFO, the FCA did not impose any additional financial penalty for the market abuse. The SFO subsequently revealed that, under the DPA, Tesco had agreed to pay a £129 million fine and £3 million in investigation costs, and undertaken to implement an ongoing compliance programme during the DPA's three year term.[77]

---

76   A DPA is a judicially supervised agreement with a corporate body allowing a prosecution to be suspended for a period of time provided the organization meets specified conditions.

77   SFO, 'Deferred Prosecution Agreement between the SFO and Tesco Published' (News Release, 23 January 2019); https://www.sfo.gov.uk/2019/01/23/deferred-prosecution-agreement-between-the-sfo-and-tesco-published/

CHAPTER 7

Evidential Perspectives

Introduction

Proving market manipulation in a forensic environment is inherently difficult. Establishing some of the criminal offences set out under Part VII FSA 2012 can be particularly challenging because they require that the prosecution prove intent. As already noted, it can be very hard to establish someone's state of mind, especially to the criminal standard, solely via inferences drawn from their trading patterns, *unless* these are extreme (albeit this is sometimes the case with HFT). A 'smoking gun' may be found, for example, in a preserved email or telephone recording that is highly incriminating, an accomplice willing to give evidence for the Crown, or a confession. In the absence of this, however, even suspiciously large trading volumes, in particular securities, at specific and sensitive times of the working day, may not be enough to make out an offence. This is especially true if the suspected person provides a vaguely plausible explanation for the transaction. Establishing manipulation in regulatory actions is simpler, but still not necessarily straightforward.

Of course, many cases involving alleged market manipulation throw up the same types of evidential problem as any other criminal or regulatory offence. For example, in *Hayes*, several of the grounds of appeal involved technical discussion of statutory exceptions to the hearsay rule. In particular, it was argued that the trial judge had wrongly refused to admit hearsay evidence, pursuant to section 117 or section 114(1)(d) of the Criminal Justice Act 2003, about conclusions reached during internal disciplinary proceedings regarding a third party. Given that market manipulators are sometimes serial offenders, the adducing of bad character evidence in the form of previous market misconduct might also become relevant.

Nevertheless, certain evidential issues found in manipulation cases are worthy of specialist consideration. Some of these have already been considered in a related context in *The Little Book of Insider Dealing*[1] and will not be repeated here. Others, such as the impact of SOCPA agreements and reverse onus defences, have already been discussed in earlier chapters of this work. However, some other issues bear closer scrutiny, especially in the light of recent cases.

Burden and Standard of Proof in Regulatory Actions

Burden of Proof

The general rule as to the incidence of the burden of proof is that he or she who asserts must prove.[2] Normally, the person deemed to be asserting in a civil matter is the claimant, and so proof of the essential elements of a civil action rest there.[3] So, too, in a criminal trial, the burden rests on the prosecution to establish the elements of the offences charged, and to disprove any defences raised (albeit to the higher standard of beyond reasonable doubt). Nevertheless, sometimes a defendant is deemed to be asserting, and so the onus of proof lies upon them on that particular issue. Thus, for example, a civil defendant who seeks to rely on an exclusion clause normally has the onus of proving that they fall within its terms.[4] In the criminal context, a defendant will generally carry only an evidential burden to raise a defence (that is, to ensure a defence is raised on the evidence, from whichever party that derives).[5] However, where the offence is a relatively minor or regulatory crime, or in the case of particular statutory defences the defendant may carry the legal burden of actually proving the elements of the defence on the balance of probabilities.[6]

In the context of regulatory proceedings for market manipulation, the

---

[1]   These include, for example, the typical professional defendant's entitlement to a full good character direction, as set out in *Vye* [1993] 1 WLR 471.

[2]   *Robins v National Trust Co Ltd* [1927] AC 515, PC.

[3]   *Chapman v Oakleigh Animal Products Ltd* (1970) 8 KIR 1063 at 1072.

[4]   *The Glendarroch* [1894] P 226.

[5]   *Lambert* [2001] UKHL 37; [2002] 2 AC 545.

[6]   See *Edwards* [1975] 1 QB 27; *Hunt* [1987] AC 352; *Carr-Briant* [1943] KB 603.

FCA is bringing the action and so it is fundamental that it must prove its case.[7] Nonetheless, it will be for a defendant to establish matters of excuse. For example, under article 12(1)(ii) MAR, market manipulation includes, *inter alia*, securing the price of financial instruments at an abnormal or artificial level, *unless* the person entering into the transaction establishes that this has been carried out for legitimate reasons, and conforms with an accepted market practice as established in article 13 MAR. Thus, on this issue, it appears to be for the defendant to prove that, on the balance of probabilities, they fall within the exception. This is the same as in the pre-MAR context, as illustrated by the *Da Vinci Invest* case. There, it was common ground between the FCA and the defendant that section 123(2) FSMA operated as a defence, and that the burden fell upon the defendant to satisfy the FCA or a tribunal of its requirements.[8]

Standard of Proof

In a regulatory action for market manipulation, the standard of proof is the civil standard of 'balance of probabilities' or 'more probable than not', both for the FCA and, where they carry the legal burden, the defendant.[9] It has also been clarified relatively recently, that this standard does not vary according to the seriousness of the allegations, a notion that held sway for a period up to the early 21st century.[10]

This was somewhat belatedly accepted by the Upper Tribunal in *Hannam v FCA* [2014] UKUT 0233 (TCC), which abandoned its previous notion of quasi-criminal standards applying in regulatory proceedings for market abuse. The tribunal concluded instead that the ordinary civil standard of the balance of probabilities should be employed, however grave the allegation.

Nevertheless, in both *Re D* and *Re B* the House of Lords had also accepted the earlier, moderating analysis of Lord Nicholls in *Re H* [1996] 1 All ER 1. There, his Lordship observed that courts could, in some circumstances,

---

7   *Hoodless and Blackwell v FSA* [2003] FSMT 007 at 20.

8   See *FCA v Da Vinci Invest Ltd* [2015] EWHC 2401 (Ch).

9   *Chhabra and Patel v FSAu* [2009] FSMT 072 at 54.

10   See the decisions of the House of Lords in *Re D (Secretary of State for Northern Ireland Intervening)* [2008] 1 WLR 1499 ('*Re D*') and *Re B (Children FC)* [2008] 3 WLR 1 ('*Re B*').

consider as a factor that the more serious an allegation is, the less likely it may be that it has occurred. Hence, his Lordship went on, 'the stronger should be the evidence before the court concludes that the allegation is established on the balance of probability'.[11] According to this analysis, it is inherently less likely that someone of previous good character with a career to lose will commit a serious crime than, for example, that they will be negligent. Such circumstances might sometimes therefore warrant an enhanced level of evidence to be provided before even the civil standard can be considered as met.

This reasoning was accepted by the predecessor to the UT(TCC) in *Chhabra and Patel v FSAu* [2009] FSMT 072. There it was observed that: 'The more inherently unlikely it is that something has happened the more persuasive the tribunal will need to find the evidence pointing that way before concluding it to be more likely than not'. However, as Snowden J observed in the market manipulation case of *Da Vinci Invest*, Lord Nicholls was not laying down a rule of law in *Re H*. Rather, there is only one rule, 'namely that the occurrence of the fact in issue must be proved to have been more probable than not. Common sense, not law, requires that in deciding this question, regard should be had, to whatever extent appropriate, to inherent probabilities'.[12] In some situations, the gravity of the allegation might be an important factor; in others, it may be totally irrelevant.

Despite the foregoing, it bears noting that regulatory proceedings for market manipulation are neither distinctly civil nor criminal. The regulatory offences were deliberately established outside the criminal sphere to enable the relevant conduct to be pursued more easily, without the strictures of a criminal trial (see *Chapter 6*). Nonetheless, regulatory proceedings are brought by an arm of the state *qua* state and involve findings of wrongdoing against individuals in a manner that may have serious consequences.

For these reasons, some would argue that the civil standard of proof is too low, and that charges should be established beyond reasonable doubt. One recent decision suggests that both the UT(TCC) and the Court of Appeal have some sympathy with that view. *Burns v FCA* [2017] EWCA

---

11   *Re B* [2008] 3 WLR 1.

12   See *FCA v Da Vinci Invest Ltd* [2015] EWHC 2401 (Ch).

Civ 2140 concerned the duties owed by the directors of limited companies and building societies under sections 175 and 177 of the Companies Act 2006, and section 63 of the Building Societies Act 1986. It was alleged that the appellant had recklessly and in breach of her fiduciary position as a non-executive director failed to disclose conflicts of interest and had used her positions to further her own commercial interests. These were serious allegations and were very vehemently denied.

After the RDC process, the matter was referred to the UT(TCC).[13] From there it went to the Court of Appeal, which reiterated that, 'where, as here, an allegation is of a particularly serious nature, the FCA must well know that it will require evidence of commensurate cogency to make it good'. This was not present in the instant case.[14] Although the simple civil standard of proof remains applicable, such comments may be persuasive in regulatory proceedings against persons of good character where evidence against them is not clearly overwhelming.

Expert Evidence

Market manipulation and the economic systems within which it is perpetrated are beyond the day-to-day experience of most individuals. Expert evidence may therefore often be of assistance to aid the understanding of the trier of fact, whether the RDC or UT(TCC) for a regulatory offence, or a jury in a criminal trial. Both prosecution/regulator and defence can tender such evidence.

Expert evidence refers to evidence not only of personal observations, to which any witness may attest, but also of the individual's opinions, where that individual is especially knowledgeable (or *peritus*) in the field that calls for such assistance. This status can normally be acquired by formal study and qualification, by practical experience, or, most commonly, by a combination of the two.[15]

Such evidence will often come from individuals with professional qualifications relevant to the finance industry, as well as considerable practical

---

13   See *Burns v FCA (formerly FSAu)* [2014] UKUT 509 (TCC) and [2015] UKUT 0601 (TCC).

14   *Burns v FCA* [2017] EWCA Civ 2140, 185.

15   See *Hodges* [2003] EWCA Crim 290.

experience as, for example, a stockbroker or compliance officer. A selection of cases is illustrative as to the diversity of matters on which expert evidence may admissible and who can be granted expert status.

One example is the *Da Vinci Invest* case, in which the FCA called Oliver Linton, a Professor of Political Economy at the University of Cambridge. His evidence dealt with the statistical probability of trading activities by the defendants having demonstrated multiple features of an abusive trading pattern discernible in a random sample in their trades. Professor Linton concluded with 95% confidence that over 90% of the incidents of trading during 2010 and 2011 before the court would have evinced those features, and with 75% confidence that 95% of them fell into that category. This evidence assisted the panel to find the regulatory offences of market abuse to be proven.

A different example of the use of expert evidence is the case of *Geddis v FSAu* [2011] UKUT 344 (TCC) before the Upper Tribunal. There, the FSAu called the LME's former Executive Director of Regulation and Compliance, Alan Whiting, as an expert witness. Whiting had held that post from December 1997 to July 2004, and had also acquired relevant experience in the Department of Trade and Industry. The UT(TCC) expressly noted that Whiting's report and oral evidence had been of considerable assistance, where the case was concerned with the appropriate penalty for market manipulation on the LME. The panel did caveat this, however, by noting that the nature of Whiting's experience meant his perspective differed from that of the applicant,[16] which was significant where there were questions around his state of mind and so his integrity. In consequence, the UT(TCC) found that the FCA (via the RDC) had been wrong to conclude that the applicant's conduct showed he was not a fit and proper person, and that prohibition was therefore not an appropriate response.

Moving abroad, in a regulatory action in October 2016, the New Zealand Financial Markets Authority accused a Milford Asset Management portfolio manager of market manipulation via ten trades between December 2013 and August 2014. The FCA's expert witnesses concluded that these trades did

---

16   *Geddis v FSAu* [2011] UKUT 344 (TCC) at 4.

constitute incidents of market manipulation. However, the manager called Michael Aitken, the chief executive officer of Capital Markets Cooperative Research Centre, to give evidence, *inter alia*, on tell-tale signs of market manipulation.[17] Aitken had an international reputation for his work in securities markets and for the design of surveillance software for real-time fraud detection in such markets, including the SMARTS system used by over 50 national stock exchanges. As this case suggests, regulators do not have a monopoly on expertise, and it may well be that there is disagreement among experts about certain trading behaviours.

Even if it appears expert evidence would be beneficial, questions may arise as to whether an individual may properly be called as an expert, or whether the evidence to be given falls within the scope of their purported expertise. Although an opposing party will often accept that a proposed expert is properly qualified (where the basis for this is made clear), that is not inevitably the case. Where questions of qualification arise, they are questions of law for the tribunal to decide, on the basis of written or oral evidence-in-chief as to their qualifications, cross-examination by the opposing party, and oral argument. The tribunal must then decide whether to admit the expert evidence in its entirety; wholly to refuse it; or to admit it on certain issues but not on others (for example, because the proposed evidence is outside the established field of expertise).

Although strict rules of evidence do not apply in proceedings before the UT(TCC),[18] general requirements for the validity of expert evidence are still respected. For example, in *Pottage v FSAu* (UKUT, FS/2010/33, April 2012) the applicant referred an FSAu decision to penalise him pursuant to section 66 FSMA to the UT(TCC). In unanimously upholding his application, the panel observed that one of the experts called by the FSAu 'might have stepped beyond his role as an expert witness'. Moreover, certain conclusions he had expressed were 'largely outside the role of expert evidence' and instead were 'trespassing on the position of the Tribunal' to make findings

---

17   'FMA's Case Is "Speculation, Supposition, and Retrospective Hindsight"—[E] Defence Opens', *NZ Herald*, 10 October 2016; https://www.nzherald.co.nz/business/news/article.cfm?c_id=3&objectid=11726199

18   See Tribunal Procedure (Upper Tribunal) Rules 2008, rule 15(1).

in order to determine the reference.[19]

In a criminal trial, the rules are of course much stricter. Part 19 of the Criminal Procedure Rules 2015 (Crim PR), as well as Criminal Practice Directions 19A to 19C, govern expert evidence in criminal matters, whether in the magistrates' courts, Crown Court or Court of Appeal. Crim PR Part 19.2 makes clear that an expert's first duty is to the court, rather than the party calling them. Experts must, *inter alia*, provide opinions that are objective, unbiased, and within their areas of expertise. Experts are therefore obliged to define the scope of their expertise in the written report that must be served in advance of the relevant hearing,[20] and in their oral evidence. When giving evidence, experts must also draw the court's attention to any question where the answer would be outside their area of expertise, or any change of opinion on their part. (Part 35 of the Civil Procedure Rules provides in an equivalent manner for expert evidence in, *inter alia*, the High Court and the civil division of the Court of Appeal).

The cornerstone of admissibility of any evidence is that it is relevant to a question to be decided by the relevant tribunal. Expert evidence must also be necessary to assist the tribunal of fact to understand matters outside their daily experience. Otherwise, it will not be allowed, or will be disregarded if called. For example, in *Legal & General Assurance Society Limited v FSAu* [2005] FSMT 015, the FSMT noted that its three members had placed little weight on expert evidence when evaluating forms and written guidance intended for consumers. This was because these were simply 'matters on which, given the background of two of us in financial services and all of us as consumers, we feel able and obliged to form our own views of the evidence'. This was, in effect, an application of principles of judicial notice, whereby members of a tribunal of fact may 'take into consideration matters which they know of their own knowledge, and particularly matters in regard to the locality', albeit not where this would be contrary to

---

19   At 178. It bears noting, however, that the rule whereby an expert may not express an opinion on the ultimate issue for determination by the tribunal of fact has been abolished in civil cases (see section 3(1) Civil Evidence Act 1972) and is not strictly applied in criminal cases (see e.g. *Hodges* [2003] EWCA Crim 290).

20   See rules 19.3(3) and 19.4 regarding the requirements around expert reports.

the evidence presented.[21]

Although expert evidence may generally appear useful in market manipulation cases, it may equally be worth considering whether such evidence is properly admissible — because, for example, it is not relevant or is beyond any expertise of the witness. An example of this may be seen in the SFO case of *Pabon*.[22] Pabon, a derivatives trader, was prosecuted for conspiracy to defraud by means of dishonestly rigging LIBOR. Five other men (making a total of six) were similarly charged, one of whom pleaded guilty, while Pabon and two others were convicted at trial. However, two defendants were acquitted on retrial after their initial jury could not agree on the verdicts.

Significantly, when the latter pair were retried, a defence request for disclosure revealed that the main expert witness called by the prosecution had given evidence beyond his general knowledge of banking. Both during the retrial and at the first trial, he had dealt with specific topics outside his area of expertise, particularly in relation to short-term interest rate trades. Although the 'expert' had some general banking and finance experience and expertise, he had never worked as an interest rate derivatives trader, a cash desk trader or a LIBOR submitter, and therefore had no direct knowledge of these areas. Furthermore, he had not worked as a trader of any kind since 2000 and, from 2005 onwards, had acted as a professional expert witness in general banking disputes. Even more alarmingly, it was revealed that, in drafting his expert report and preparing for trial, he had sought and obtained significant assistance from friends, and that he continued to do this during the course of giving his evidence.[23] The Court of Appeal subsequently identified numerous other serious failings in his evidence.

The expert's status and evidence constituted the sole ground of appeal advanced by Pabon, who argued that the fresh evidence concerning his shortcomings would have permitted devastating cross-examination at his own trial, had it been known about at the time. Consequently, he asserted, his conviction was unsafe.

The Court of Appeal rejected the appeal, on the basis that there was no

---

21 *Ingram v Percival* [1969] 1 QB 548 at 555 (Lord Parker CJ).

22 See *Pabon* [2018] EWCA Crim 420.

23 Ibid at paras 43–49.

causal link between the tendered expert's failings and the ensuing conviction: the issue at trial had simply been whether or not Pabon had acted dishonestly. He had admitted seeking to move the LIBOR rate to suit his trading book and to favour his bank and trading team, such that the conviction was not unsafe.

Nevertheless, the Court of Appeal accepted that there were numerous deficiencies around the expert's evidence, describing the SFO's decision to instruct him as an 'embarrassing debacle'.[24] In other circumstances, these failings may well have been fatal to a conviction. The Court of Appeal recognised that questions as to his expertise had not previously arisen but emphasised 'the need for those instructing expert witnesses to satisfy themselves as to a witness' expertise and to engage (difficult though it sometimes may be) an expert of a suitable calibre'.

Evidently, the Court of Appeal was not ignorant of the difficulty in identifying an appropriate expert in such arcane and recondite cases, albeit making clear that this was not a reason for accepting a lesser standard of ability.[25] Numerous informed observers have reiterated this difficulty.[26] Even extensive general experience of the financial markets as, for example, with a broker, may not be enough to equip someone to venture an opinion on the more obscure aspects of dealing. In these settings, the use of niche (former) practitioners to explain market practice has become increasingly important. Perhaps indicative of the degree of specialism involved in such cases is the SFO's alleged (it has not been confirmed) dealing with Tom Hayes in 2013. At that time, Hayes was co-operating with the SFO pursuant to a SOCPA agreement for his own LIBOR fixing activities. Nonetheless, the SFO reportedly considered instructing him as an expert witness in other LIBOR prosecutions totally unrelated to Hayes, because he was one of very

---

24 Ibid at para 76.

25 The ongoing challenges of finding appropriate experts in novel areas around financial markets may also be indicated by the CPS' recent abandonment of a trial for conspiracy to defraud in connection with investments in carbon credits: see e.g. Owen Bowcott, 'Fraud Trial Abandoned Because Expert Witness Had No Expertise', *The Guardian*, 29 May 2019; https://www.theguardian.com/law/2019/may/29/trial-abandoned-because-expert-witness-had-no-expertise

26 David Kirk, 'Enforcement of Criminal Sanctions for Market Abuse: Practicalities, Problem Solving and Pitfalls' (2016) 17(3) *ERA Forum* 311–322 at 318.

few people who would know about its more complex features.[27] Ultimately, however, the basis for his expertise may also have been the reason for his abandonment as a candidate.

Similarly, in July 2018, the SFO abandoned a criminal enquiry into possible LIBOR rigging by traders at Lloyds Banking Group because the case had not met the threshold required for prosecution. It was reported that one reason behind this was the difficulty in finding an expert willing and able to provide evidence regarding the traders' behaviour, especially after the controversy in *Pabon*.[28]

---

27 David Enrich, *The Spider Network* (2018, HarperCollins) at 367.

28 Harry Wilson, 'Fraud Office Drops Lloyds Libor Investigation', *The Times*, 4 July 2018; https://www.thetimes.co.uk/article/lloyds-libor-investigation-dropped-by-fraud-office-mlc3gj7l5

CHAPTER 8

Conclusion

In the modern era, market manipulation can come in many forms. However, it is its more sophisticated manifestations that occasion most problems. For a wrong that almost began life with groups of men dressed up in Bourbon uniforms spreading false information in cod French accents, market manipulation has come a very long way. The speed of change has accelerated dramatically over the past two decades, with the advent of the Internet, novel forms of electronic communication, ultra-fast computer-generated dealing, new types of financial instrument, and the increased globalisation of markets. All of these factors provide the means and opportunities for carrying out new forms of manipulation on ever-larger scales.

The US SEC's Division of Enforcement remarked upon this change at the end of 2017, noting that: 'Just a few years ago, it was difficult to imagine a market manipulation scheme accomplished by hacking into the electronic accounts of others and then forcing trades to pump up a stock price'. Yet by then, such schemes were being encountered on a fairly regular basis.[1]

Even more drastic change is on its way. In early 2019, the FCA's Director of Enforcement noted that markets are on the brink of the quantum-computing era.[2] With that development, increases in the speed and quantities in which data processing may occur will be immense.

Inevitably, financial authorities throughout the world struggle to keep up with technological advances. It is difficult to draft legislation that can deal effectively with future market and technological changes, and even harder to monitor relevant information within the wider and ever-growing torrent of trading data that modern firms generate on a daily basis. Even as stricter

---

1   US SEC Division of Enforcement, *Annual Report: A Look Back at Fiscal Year 2017* (2017); https://www.sec.gov/files/enforcement-annual-report-2017.pdf at 2.

2   Hoggett, 'Dynamic Response'.

regulation and surveillance is introduced, the goalposts continue to shift.

Of course, as with any type of wrongful conduct, the incidence of market misconduct can be reduced but never wholly eradicated.[3] Nevertheless, a regulatory system that relies on detecting when abuse has occurred will never be as effective as one that also helps prevent it in the first place. In this regard, the FCA's emphasis, following MAR's introduction, on prevention via improved monitoring appears to be bearing fruit. Indicia of this are the number of STORs submitted and the increased investment by financial sector firms in market-monitoring software. It is to be hoped that further efforts in this direction continue.

It will also be interesting to see how the criminal and regulatory frameworks continue to develop in enforcement. In the UK, the respective merits of each have been explored, and their relative fortunes as a way of dealing with manipulation have ebbed and flowed. Certainly, the increased complexity and sophistication of many manipulation cases may be challenging for lay jurors. The lesser mental element required for many regulatory offences, the lower standard of proof, the use of tribunals with specialist expertise, and the fact that very significant punishments can be imposed, mean that the regulatory route has many attractions for authorities. Nonetheless, where the evidential and public interest thresholds are met, criminal prosecutions will and should continue: the impact of market misconduct can be vast and deeply-felt across all levels of society, and should not be treated as less serious simply because the harm is financial rather than physical (unlike theft).

Globalisation is a further feature rendering market manipulation difficult to tackle. This is only increasing and so it is clear that, more than ever before, national regulators need to cooperate in the detection and investigation of cross-border manipulation. Robust domestic capacities are also key to these efforts, both at home and abroad.

Nevertheless, it is also important to note that, despite the high level of change seen in recent years, certain themes persist, as they have done for centuries, giving market manipulation a considerable degree of continuity.

---

3   Mark Steward, 'Has the Industry Improved Ten Years On?' (speech delivered at the Banking Litigation and Regulation Forum, London, 14 June 2018); https://www.fca.org.uk/news/speeches/has-industry-improved-ten-years

It is vital to remember that the ideas are not new, even if their particular application might be. Boiled down to their essence, they are often fairly straightforward.[4]

Most importantly, the vast majority of manipulation cases still involve the dissemination of false information or the commission of misleading acts, just as they did when Joseph de la Vega was trading on the Amsterdam Stock Exchange in the late 1600s. The means by which this is done may have been transformed, but the effect on investors who are eager to seek out a profit, while being fearful of sustaining a loss, is and probably always will be, the same.

---

4   Hoggett, 'Dynamic Response'.

Frequently Used Acronyms

AIM	Alternative Investment Market
AFME	Association for Financial Markets in Europe
BoE	Bank of England
CFD	Contract for difference
CSMAD	Criminal Sanctions for Market Abuse Directive
CPS	Crown Prosecution Service
DEPP	Decision Procedure and Penalties Manual
ECHR	European Convention of Human Rights
EMO	Enforcement and Market Oversight Division
ESMA	European Securities and Markets Authority
EURIBOR	European Inter Bank Offered Rate
FCA	Financial Conduct Authority
FICC	Fixed Income, Currencies and Commodities
FMSB	FICC Market Standards Board
FSA 1986	Financial Services Act 1986
FSA 2012	Financial Services Act 2012
FSAu	Financial Services Authority
FSMA	Financial Services and Markets Act 2000
FX	Foreign exchange (sometimes Forex)
LIBOR	London Inter Bank Offered Rate
LIFFE	London International Financial Future and Options Exchange
LSE	London Stock Exchange
MAR	Market Abuse Regulation (EU) No. 596/2014, as amended
MAD	Market Abuse Directive
MTF	Multilateral Trading Facility
OTF	Organised Trading Facility
PACE	Police and Criminal Evidence Act 1984

PRA	Prudential Regulation Authority
RNS	Regulatory News Service
RDC	Regulatory Decisions Committee
SEC	US Securities and Exchange Commission
SFO	Serious Fraud Office
SOCPA	Serious Organised Crime and Police Act 2005
STOR	Suspicious Transaction and Order Report
STR	Suspicious Transaction Report
UT(TCC)	Upper Tribunal (Tax and Chancery Chamber)

Financial Services Act 2012 (Extract)

PART 7 Offences relating to financial services

89 Misleading statements

(1) Subsection (2) applies to a person ('P') who —

    (a) makes a statement which P knows to be false or misleading in a material respect,

    (b) makes a statement which is false or misleading in a material respect, being reckless as to whether it is, or

    (c) dishonestly conceals any material facts whether in connection with a statement made by P or otherwise.

(2) P commits an offence if P makes the statement or conceals the facts with the intention of inducing, or is reckless as to whether making it or concealing them may induce, another person (whether or not the person to whom the statement is made)—

    (a) to enter into or offer to enter into, or to refrain from entering or offering to enter into, a relevant agreement, or

    (b) to exercise, or refrain from exercising, any rights conferred by a relevant investment.

(3) In proceedings for an offence under subsection (2) brought against a person to whom that subsection applies as a result of paragraph (a) of subsection (1), it is a defence for the person charged ('D') to show that the statement was made in conformity with—

    (a) price stabilising rules,

    (b) control of information rules, or

(c)   the relevant provisions of Commission Regulation (EC) No. 2273/2003 of 22 December 2003 implementing Directive 2003/6/EC of the European Parliament and of the Council as regards exemptions for buy-back programmes and stabilisation of financial instruments.

(4)   Subsections (1) and (2) do not apply unless—

(a)   the statement is made in or from, or the facts are concealed in or from, the United Kingdom or arrangements are made in or from the United Kingdom for the statement to be made or the facts to be concealed,

(b)   the person on whom the inducement is intended to or may have effect is in the United Kingdom, or

(c)   the agreement is or would be entered into or the rights are or would be exercised in the United Kingdom.

90 Misleading impressions

(1)   A person ('P') who does any act or engages in any course of conduct which creates a false or misleading impression as to the market in or the price or value of any relevant investments commits an offence if—

(a)   P intends to create the impression, and

(b)   the case falls within subsection (2) or (3) (or both).

(2)   The case falls within this subsection if P intends, by creating the impression, to induce another person to acquire, dispose of, subscribe for or underwrite the investments or to refrain from doing so or to exercise or refrain from exercising any rights conferred by the investments.

(3)   The case falls within this subsection if—

(a)   P knows that the impression is false or misleading or is reckless as to whether it is, and

(b)   P intends by creating the impression to produce any of the results in subsection (4) or is aware that creating the impression is likely to produce any of the results in that subsection.

(4)   Those results are—
    (a)   the making of a gain for P or another, or
    (b)   the causing of loss to another person or the exposing of another person to the risk of loss.

(5)   References in subsection (4) to gain or loss are to be read in accordance with subsections (6) to (8).

(6)   'Gain' and 'loss'—
    (a)   extend only to gain or loss in money or other property of any kind;
    (b)   include such gain or loss whether temporary or permanent.

(7)   'Gain' includes a gain by keeping what one has, as well as a gain by getting what one does not have.

(8)   'Loss' includes a loss by not getting what one might get, as well as a loss by parting with what one has.

(9)   In proceedings brought against any person ('D') for an offence under subsection (1) it is a defence for D to show—
    (a)   to the extent that the offence results from subsection (2), that D reasonably believed that D's conduct would not create an impression that was false or misleading as to the matters mentioned in subsection (1),
    (b)   that D acted or engaged in the conduct—
        (i) for the purpose of stabilising the price of investments, and
        (ii) in conformity with price stabilising rules,
    (c)   that D acted or engaged in the conduct in conformity with control of information rules, or
    (d)   that D acted or engaged in the conduct in conformity with the relevant provisions of Commission Regulation (EC) No. 2273/2003 of 22 December 2003 implementing Directive 2003/6/EC of the European Parliament and of the Council as regards exemptions for buy-back programmes and stabilisation of financial instruments.

(10)   This section does not apply unless—

    (a)   the act is done, or the course of conduct is engaged in, in the United Kingdom, or

    (b)   the false or misleading impression is created there.

91 Misleading statements etc. in relation to benchmarks

(1)   A person ('A') who makes to another person ('B') a false or misleading statement commits an offence if—

    (a)   A makes the statement in the course of arrangements for the setting of a relevant benchmark,

    (b)   A intends that the statement should be used by B for the purpose of the setting of a relevant benchmark, and

    (c)   A knows that the statement is false or misleading or is reckless as to whether it is.

(2)   A person ('C') who does any act or engages in any course of conduct which creates a false or misleading impression as to the price or value of any investment or as to the interest rate appropriate to any transaction commits an offence if—

    (a)   C intends to create the impression,

    (b)   the impression may affect the setting of a relevant benchmark,

    (c)   C knows that the impression is false or misleading or is reckless as to whether it is, and

    (d)   C knows that the impression may affect the setting of a relevant benchmark.

(3)   In proceedings for an offence under subsection (1), it is a defence for the person charged ('D') to show that the statement was made in conformity with—

    (a)   price stabilising rules,

    (b)   control of information rules, or

    (c)   the relevant provisions of Commission Regulation (EC) No. 2273/2003 of 22 December 2003 implementing Directive 2003/6/EC of the European Parliament and of the Council as regards exemptions for buy-back programmes and stabilisation of financial instruments.

(4)   In proceedings brought against any person ('D') for an offence under subsection (2) it is a defence for D to show—

    (a)   that D acted or engaged in the conduct—

      (i) for the purpose of stabilising the price of investments, and

      (ii) in conformity with price stabilising rules,

    (b)   that D acted or engaged in the conduct in conformity with control of information rules, or

    (c)   that D acted or engaged in the conduct in conformity with the relevant provisions of Commission Regulation (EC) No. 2273/2003 of 22 December 2003 implementing Directive 2003/6/EC of the European Parliament and of the Council as regards exemptions for buy-back programmes and stabilisation of financial instruments.

(5)   Subsection (1) does not apply unless the statement is made in or from the United Kingdom or to a person in the United Kingdom.

(6)   Subsection (2) does not apply unless—

    (a)   the act is done, or the course of conduct is engaged in, in the United Kingdom, or

    (b)   the false or misleading impression is created there.

92 Penalties

(1)   A person guilty of an offence under this Part is liable—

    (a)   on summary conviction, to imprisonment for a term not exceeding the applicable maximum term or a fine not exceeding the statutory maximum, or both;

    (b)   on conviction on indictment, to imprisonment for a term not exceeding 7 years or a fine, or both.

(2)   For the purpose of subsection (1)(a) 'the applicable maximum term' is—

(a) in England and Wales, 12 months (or 6 months, if the offence was committed before the commencement of section 154(1) of the Criminal Justice Act 2003);

(b) in Scotland, 12 months;

(c) in Northern Ireland, 6 months.

93 Interpretation of Part 7

(1) This section has effect for the interpretation of this Part.

(2) 'Investment' includes any asset, right or interest.

(3) 'Relevant agreement' means an agreement—
(a) the entering into or performance of which by either party constitutes an activity of a kind specified in an order made by the Treasury, and
(b) which relates to a relevant investment.

(4) Relevant benchmark' means a benchmark of a kind specified in an order made by the Treasury.

(5) 'Relevant investment' means an investment of a kind specified in an order made by the Treasury.

(6) Schedule 2 to FSMA 2000 (except paragraphs 25 and 26) applies for the purposes of subsections (3) and (5) with references to section 22 of that Act being read as references to each of those subsections.

(7) Nothing in Schedule 2 to FSMA 2000, as applied by subsection (6), limits the power conferred by subsection (3) or (5).

(8) 'Price stabilising rules' and 'control of information rules' have the same meaning as in FSMA 2000.

(9)   In this section 'benchmark' has the meaning given in section 22(6) of
FSMA 2000.

Market Abuse Regulation 2016 (Extract)

Article 15 Prohibition of market manipulation

A person shall not engage in or attempt to engage in market manipulation.

Article 12 Market manipulation

(1)   For the purposes of this Regulation, market manipulation shall comprise
the following activities:

   (a)   entering into a transaction, placing an order to trade or any other
behaviour which:

      (i)   gives, or is likely to give, false or misleading signals as to the
supply of, demand for, or price of, a financial instrument, a
related spot commodity contract or an auctioned product based
on emission allowances; or

      (ii) secures, or is likely to secure, the price of one or several financial
instruments, a related spot commodity contract or an auctioned
product based on emission allowances at an abnormal or artificial level; unless the person entering into a transaction, placing
an order to trade or engaging in any other behaviour establishes
that such transaction, order or behaviour have been carried out
for legitimate reasons, and conform with an accepted market
practice as established in accordance with article 13;

   (b)   entering into a transaction, placing an order to trade or any other
activity or behaviour which affects or is likely to affect the price
of one or several financial instruments, a related spot commodity
contract or an auctioned product based on emission allowances,
which employs a fictitious device or any other form of deception or
contrivance;

   (c)   disseminating information through the media, including the
internet, or by any other means, which gives, or is likely to give,

false or misleading signals as to the supply of, demand for, or price of, a financial instrument, a related spot commodity contract or an auctioned product based on emission allowances or secures, or is likely to secure, the price of one or several financial instruments, a related spot commodity contract or an auctioned product based on emission allowances at an abnormal or artificial level, including the dissemination of rumours, where the person who made the dissemination knew, or ought to have known, that the information was false or misleading;

(d) transmitting false or misleading information or providing false or misleading inputs in relation to a benchmark where the person who made the transmission or provided the input knew or ought to have known that it was false or misleading, or any other behaviour which manipulates the calculation of a benchmark.

(2) The following behaviour shall, inter alia, be considered as market manipulation:

(a) the conduct by a person, or persons acting in collaboration, to secure a dominant position over the supply of or demand for a financial instrument, related spot commodity contracts or auctioned products based on emission allowances which has, or is likely to have, the effect of fixing, directly or indirectly, purchase or sale prices or creates, or is likely to create, other unfair trading conditions;

(b) the buying or selling of financial instruments, at the opening or closing of the market, which has or is likely to have the effect of misleading investors acting on the basis of the prices displayed, including the opening or closing prices;

(c) the placing of orders to a trading venue, including any cancellation or modification thereof, by any available means of trading, including by electronic means, such as algorithmic and high-frequency trading strategies, and which has one of the effects referred to in paragraph 1(a) or (b), by:

(i) disrupting or delaying the functioning of the trading system of the trading venue or being likely to do so;

(ii) making it more difficult for other persons to identify genuine orders on the trading system of the trading venue or being likely to do so, including by entering orders which result in the overloading or destabilisation of the order book; or

(iii) creating or being likely to create a false or misleading signal about the supply of, or demand for, or price of, a financial instrument, in particular by entering orders to initiate or exacerbate a trend;

(d) the taking advantage of occasional or regular access to the traditional or electronic media by voicing an opinion about a financial instrument, related spot commodity contract or an auctioned product based on emission allowances (or indirectly about its issuer) while having previously taken positions on that financial instrument, a related spot commodity contract or an auctioned product based on emission allowances and profiting subsequently from the impact of the opinions voiced on the price of that instrument, related spot commodity contract or an auctioned product based on emission allowances, without having simultaneously disclosed that conflict of interest to the public in a proper and effective way;

(e) the buying or selling on the secondary market of emission allowances or related derivatives prior to the auction held pursuant to Regulation (EU) No. 1031/2010 with the effect of fixing the auction clearing price for the auctioned products at an abnormal or artificial level or misleading bidders bidding in the auctions.

(3) For the purposes of applying paragraph 1(a) and (b), and without prejudice to the forms of behaviour set out in paragraph 2, Annex I defines non-exhaustive indicators relating to the employment of a fictitious device or any other form of deception or contrivance, and non-exhaustive indicators related to false or misleading signals and to price securing.

(4)   Where the person referred to in this Article is a legal person, this Article shall also apply, in accordance with national law, to the natural persons who participate in the decision to carry out activities for the account of the legal person concerned.

(5)   The Commission shall be empowered to adopt delegated acts in accordance with Article 35 specifying the indicators laid down in Annex I, in order to clarify their elements and to take into account technical developments on financial markets.

Select Bibliography

Alexander, Kern, *Insider Dealing and Market Abuse: The Financial Services and Markets Act 2000* (2001) ESRC Centre for Business Research, University of Cambridge, Working Paper No. 222.

Anderson, Geraint, *Cityboy: Beer and Loathing in the Square Mile* (2009, Headline).

Anderson, Karen, et al, *A Practitioner's Guide to the Law and Regulation of Market Abuse* (2017, Sweet & Maxwell, 2nd edn).

Austin, Janet, *When Insider Trading and Market Manipulation Cross Jurisdictions. What Are the Challenges for Securities Regulators and How Can They Best Preserve the Integrity of Markets?* (2016, PhD Thesis — University of York (Toronto)); https://digitalcommons. osgoode.yorku.ca/cgi/viewcontent.cgi?referer=&httpsredir=1&article =1021&context=phd

Barnes, Paul, *Stock Market Efficiency, Insider Dealing and Market Abuse* (2009, Routledge).

Barnes, Paul, 'Insider Dealing and Market Abuse: The UK's Record on Enforcement' (2011) 39 *International Journal of Law, Crime and Justice* 174–189.

Bromberg, Lev, et al, 'The Extent and Intensity of Insider Trading Enforcement — An International Comparison' (2017) 17(1) *Journal of Corporate Law Studies* 73–110.

Fisher, Jonathan, *Fighting Fraud and Financial Crime: A New Architecture for the Investigation and Prosecution of Serious Fraud, Corruption and Financial Market Crimes* (2010) Policy Exchange Research Note; https://www.policyexchange.org.uk/wp-content/uploads/2016/09/ fighting-fraud-and-financial-crime-mar-10.pdf

Fisher, Jonathan, *Who Should Prosecute Fraud, Corruption and Financial Markets Crime?* (2013) London School of Economics, Law and

Financial Markets Project Briefing 3/13; http://www.lse.ac.uk/law/ Assets/Documents/law-and-financial-markets-project/fisher-who-should-prosecute.pdf

Fisher, Jonathan et al 'Criminal Forms of High Frequency Trading on the Financial Markets' (2015) 9(2) *Law and Financial Markets Review* 113-119

Hamer, David, 'The Presumption of Innocence and Reverse Burdens: A Balancing Act' (2007) 66 *Cambridge Law Journal* 142–171.

Harrison, Karen, and Nicholas Ryder, *The Law Relating to Financial Crime in the United Kingdom* (2013, Routledge).

Haynes, Andrew 'Market Abuse, Fraud and Misleading Communications' (2012) 19(3) *Journal of Financial Crime* 234–254.

Herlin-Karnell, Ester and Nicholas Ryder, *Market Manipulation and Insider Trading: Regulatory Challenges in the United States of America, the European Union and the United Kingdom* (2018, Hart).

Jordanoska, Aleksandra, 'Case Management in Complex Fraud Trials: Actors and Strategies in Achieving Procedural Efficiency' (2017) 13(3) *International Journal of Law in Context* 336–355.

Kirk, David, 'Enforcement of Criminal Sanctions for Market Abuse: Practicalities, Problem Solving and Pitfalls' (2016) 17(3) *ERA Forum* 311–322.

Leinweber, David, and Ananth Madhavan, 'Three Hundred Years of Stock Market Manipulation' (2001) 10(2) *The Journal of Investing* 7–16.

Macey, Jonathan R, 'Securities Trading: A Contractual Perspective' (1999) 50 *Case Western Reserve Law Review* 269–290.

Mayhew, David, *Financial Services Regulation: Challenge in The Upper Tribunal* (2012, ThirtyNine Essex Street); http://www.39essex.com/ docs/articles/challenge_in_the_tribunal_-_dm.pdf

McMullen, Clare and Elly Proudlock, 'A Review of Financial Services Enforcement and Investigation in the UK' in Marieke Breijer (ed) *The European, Middle Eastern and African Investigations Review 2018* (2018, Global Investigations Review).

Mock, Sebastian and Marco Ventoruzzo (eds), *Market Abuse Regulation:*

Commentary and Annotated Guide (2017, Oxford University Press).

Montgomery, Clare, et al (eds), *Fraud: Criminal Law and Procedure* (2015, Oxford University Press).

Planet Compliance, *The 7 Deadly Sins of Market Abuse: An Introduction to the Market Abuse Regime* (2016); https://www.planetcompliance.com/ebooks/ebook-7-deadly-sins-market-abuse/

Putnin, Talis J, 'Market Manipulation: A Survey' (2012) 26(5) *Journal of Economic Surveys* 952–967.

Rider, Barry et al, *Market Abuse and Insider Dealing* (2016, Bloomsbury Professional, 3rd ed).

Stamp, M (ed) *International Insider Dealing* (2005, City and Financial).

Wilson, Gary and Sarah Wilson, 'The FSA, "Credible Deterrence", and Criminal Enforcement—A "Haphazard Pursuit"?' (2014) 21(1) *Journal of Financial Crime* 4–28.

Wilson, Sarah, *The Origins of Modern Financial Crime: Historical Foundations and Current Problems in Britain* (2014, Routledge).

Index

The Little Book of Insider Dealing

An Essential Guide to the Law

Gregory J Durston and Mohsin Zaidi

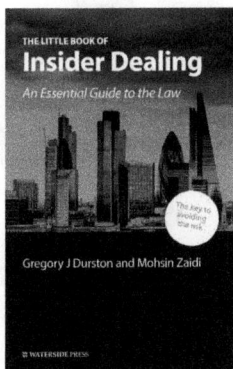

Since the Financial Crisis of 2008, criminal prosecution has become the preferred way to punish and deter the unlawful practice of trading with access to sensitive non-public information. *The Little Book of Insider Dealing* looks at the 'insider dealing' offences created by the Criminal Justice Act 1993, including their history and rationale—as well as their relationship to the overlapping civil regulatory regime that also governs this type of financial misconduct. The result is a gem of a guide to essential law around this topic, making it suitable for finance industry professionals, lawyers, students and investors needing a concise summary of the hazards involved.

'Much more than a primer [this book] provides an indispensable first and frequent point of reference for anyone dealing with this complex area of criminal law'—*John Ryder QC.*

'An extraordinarily good book…We cannot commend it highly enough'—
Phillip Taylor MBE and Elizabeth Taylor, Richmond Green Chambers.

Paperback & ebook | ISBN 978-1-909976-53-5 | 2018 | 192 pages

www.WatersidePress.co.uk